"LET'S GET CRACKING!"

The How-To Book of Bullwhip Skills

by

Robert Dante

Photographs by Chris Wiggins & Robert Dante
(With Robert Dante, Tina Nagy, Brenda Fogg and Chris Wiggins)

Library of Congress Cataloging-in-Publication Data

Dante, Robert 1953-

Let's Get Cracking! The How-To Book of Bullwhip Skills
By Robert Dante

ISBN 1440406235
EAN-13 9781440406232.
Dewey Decimal Classification 799.5

For Tina,
who beautifully and bravely
'Dances on the Edge'

4

Additional copies of this book are available for $16.95 plus shipping from www.bullwhip.biz. To order by credit card on the phone, call 831-869-1717.

CONTENTS

FORWARD

In Silverton Oregon lies Cyrus W. Barger (1847-1924), buried at his request with a whip in his hand, just as he used to hold it when he drove a stagecoach. A whip was such an important symbol of a stagecoach driver that they were called whips, just as the guard on the back was called the shotgun. It seems that old Cyrus Barger wasn't sure where he was going, but wherever it was, he thought a whip might come in handy.

There is something about a good whip that makes you not want to let go, in Cyrus's case even after he had let go of life itself. A whip has its own life, its own spirit, its own energy. Like a fine sports car or a racing yacht, a good whip can be both a work of art and a perfect machine. If you read this book carefully, you will see that it is about more than just the mechanics of cracking a whip. It is about the spirit of the whip itself.

Does this sound too philosophical? Well, never mind, the way of the whip is a pragmatic one, too, with tangles or welts to punish misjudgment, and a perfect crisp clear crack when you find the true path. And what better guide could you have on this path than Robert Dante?

If you watch Robert cracking a whip you will see the same grace and economy of motion as Tai Chi master. The whip and the wielder move as a single organism, in sensuous curves punctuated by vibrant cracks. Such apparent ease is the product of years of dedicated practice and study. In this book, Robert shares what he has learned in those years. Of course, you still have quite a bit of practice ahead of you before you are as good as he is, but it will be easier for you than it was for him as you have his experience to help you.

Welcome, everyone, to the magic of Robert Dante.

Andrew Conway
Author of "The Bullwhip Book"

8

Ch. 1 – The Preliminaries

Safety First – Learning the Lingo – Can Kids Learn to Crack Whips? – Getting Started – The Source of Your Whip's Power – Whip Anatomy 101 – Belly Up to the Bar, Boys! – Inside the Tracks, Outside the Tracks –- Hand Position (Vee is for Victory) – Practicing with Both Hands

---

Safety First

When you were born, the Universe gave you two eyes. You don't get any more.

So first things first: **Protect your eyes!**

Wear safety goggles or glasses, especially when you are practicing new moves.

I have seen experienced whip crackers catch themselves. I saw one man almost lose an eye when a slippery floor resulted in the whip being misaligned behind him at the start of a throw with an unfamiliar whip. This was a fellow who'd been cracking for years and knew what he was doing, so imagine the odds you will be on the receiving end of an errant throw when you are just starting out.

Wear a hat with a wide brim. This will catch the whip when it comes back to slash your face, and it will protect your ears. You don't want to sport that bandage-eared Van Gogh look at your next party!

Even with a wide-brimmed hat and safety goggles, you may still catch one across the face, so if you are sensitive about your looks (or if, like actors, you make your living with your appearance), do not be ashamed to don a hockey helmet with a visor. A whip travels a lot faster than a puck. If you're really worried, you can buy a hard hat made for chainsaw users. This inexpensive head covering has ear protection and a wire mesh faceplate. A motorcycle helmet also can give you full head protection.

If your ears are sensitive or if you are working in a loud, echoing place like a squash court or dance studio, wear ear plugs. Even legendary Lash LaRue complained that his whip made one ear partially deaf.

Wear long pants and long sleeves. Even plain cotton can mitigate a painful whack. Beginners particularly will slash their arms and legs. A shirt will not stop you from being hit by a good smack, but it may soften a cutting stroke. It won't remove the risk entirely.

Leather, of course, will protect you well.

Curiously, most serious accidents I have seen are because the whip handler's focus wandered more than because he or she was a beginner.

Beginners who are nervous about the whip will err on the side of caution. After cracking for a little while, they gain confidence. They think they can perform new moves and try harder combinations. They forget the basics. That's when the whip punishes them for not paying attention.

An analogy to motorcycle riding holds true here. Most accidents occur from six months to one year when the rider has just enough experience to become slightly overconfident. Most accidents occur in parking lots below 30 mph, with a car cutting in front of a bike at a 45-degree angle because it didn't see the rider. It's the simplest, most mundane moments that are most fraught with danger. Remember this the next time you wonder if you can go from a straight ahead Circus Crack directly into a Volley.

If you are cracking outside, be especially cautious if the wind is rising. An ill-timed gust can catch the fall and cracker and throw your aim off.

Safety is no joke. Being careful is not a sign that you don't know what you're doing. It doesn't mean you're a coward. Being conscious of the potential for unplanned damage means you DO know what the whip is capable of doing to yourself and to others. Govern yourself accordingly.

Every whip has essentially this anatomy: a handle, a thong, a fall and a cracker. Don't worry, because we'll expand definitions shortly.

The handle transfers the force of the throw into the thong, creating a loop which travels the length of the whip. As the loop in the thong moves away from the thrower, the loop becomes smaller, concentrating the whip's kinetic energy and making the thong accelerate until it breaks the sound barrier at the end of the whip. This is the crack.

A whip's crack truly is the sound of the cracker passing the sound barrier at 761 miles per hour. That's 10 times faster than the highest speed allowed on a freeway. That's faster than most passenger jets. A stronger crack may achieve a speed in excess of 900 miles per hour.

To give you an idea of how fast this is, understand that the speed of sound is 1400 feet per second. A bullet fired from a 44- caliber Magnum leaves the gun's barrel at 1100 feet per second. This means that a bullwhip's crack is faster than a speeding bullet.

Back in Annie Oakley's day, a bullet left the barrel of a rifle at about 850 feet per second.

For the scientists among you, if you'd like to see photos of the mini-sonic booms created by a popper as it hits Mach 1, there is an article titled "On the Dynamics of a Bullwhip" which appeared in the Journal of the Acoustical Society of America (Vol. 30, No. 12), published in December 1958.

According to Andrew Conway, author of "The Bullwhip Book," there are further references to scientific papers about bullwhips in Wolfgang Schebeczek's bibliographic notes in Kaskade No. 42, published in the summer of 1996.

Learning the Lingo

Just as beginners can become bewildered by the lack of common terms for identical cracks and whips, they may also be baffled when they encounter the same word being used to describe different things.

Take a deep breath and accept that you will always be wrong in someone else's eyes. This should not stop you. You're in good company.

For example, a whip's fall can be either an Australian style (a long, sinuous, rounded 'shoelace' attached to the thong) or a Texas style (a flat 'slapper' which is an extension of the thong itself). They are both falls.

The end of the handle is called the Turk's Head (when it is a braided ball covering the end of the handle. It can also be called the butt of the whip, or the knob, or the knot.

At the other end of the whip, that tasseled string tied to the fall is called the cracker. In some circles, it is called the popper. Some folks call it the lash. They are all correct.

Starting to get the idea? Sometimes, it's like trying to find a seat at the Mad Hatter's tea party. Don't worry about it. Just accept that all roads lead to Rome. Develop a healthy sense of humor. I guarantee that you will hear experienced whip crackers occasionally josh each other on this issue ("Say, was that a flick or an overhand throw?" "Yep!").

Can Kids Learn To Crack Whips?

If kids can learn karate or other "adult" sports, they can also learn to handle bullwhips and stock whips safely and expertly.

Some of the best whip crackers in history were smaller men and women. To crack a whip powerfully, accurately and dramatically does not require a great deal of strength. If the form is correct, the physics of the whip will allow the cracker to reach supersonic speeds with relatively little effort.

In Australia, kids enter junior whip handling competitions at county fairs. I have several videos of this. Mike Murphy, the world famous whip maker and whip cracker, sells a video showing Andrew Thomas, the champion whip cracker, performing routines with an 8-year old Daniel Wicks doing precisely the same moves right beside him. Yes, the boy's whips are shorter, but he holds his own. He will be a great ambassador for whip cracking in the future!

The United States is far behind Australia in this sport, but interest is growing. Since the Australians have codified criteria for objectively judging whip routines and competitions, the back-scene buzz is that someday whip cracking will be an Olympic sport.

What are the benefits such instruction can give a child? Just as many as karate or soccer can offer a kid!

A youngster's confidence grows as he or she sees that the whip will crack, almost magically, by itself. This is a lot of power for a child to control, the sort of thing kids have been jazzed about for years.

In the Victorian era, children used whips to keep tops spinning as a game. Even today, if I practice in a park, it's the little ones who drag their parents over to watch!

Whip cracking teaches youngsters to have confidence, self discipline, the philosophy of "less is more," and an understanding of logical consequences. It gives a sense of camaraderie to youths – once a child masters a move they first desire to show off. They then try to teach the move to others.

In many ways it is easier to teach kids than adults. Kids don't intellectualize what they're doing. They just do it.

To get adults into this open-minded "child's" way of learning, I have them work with their weaker hands where they are more awkward. This forces them to listen to their bodies and to pay attention to the reality of the moment like children. They are less likely to compare what's happening with some ideal image of how things "ought" to be. When they go back to using their dominant hands, they are amazed to see how much their weaker hands have taught them.

People enjoy this as a sport for its own sake, feeling the satisfaction of resounding and graceful cracks coming from the whips in their hands.

People still enjoy the sport of archery, although we no longer have to kill wild game to eat. We enjoy martial arts like karate and kendo, though the age of the samurai is past. And while there aren't too many cattle drives through the hearts of cities, anymore, there are whip cracking clubs in urban areas. Cracking whips makes kids of us all, so it's natural that kids enjoy this sport!

Getting Started – Overview

First learn how to hold your whip, then how to create "safe zones," and then how to throw the three basic cracks. With these tools, you can learn more advanced cracking routines, combinations and tricks.

14

The Source of Your Whip's Power

All whip cracks are variations on one movement. A whip cracks because as a loop traveling along a thong becomes smaller, the traveling loop's speed increases as it approaches the end of the thong.

Large circle rolls along thong

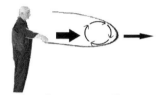

As circle travels, it becomes smaller

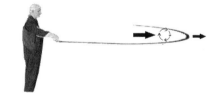

As circle becomes smaller, it spins faster

The best analogy is that of the spinning ice skater who rotates at a specific speed when her arms are outstretched. As she pulls her arms in closer to her body, her rotational speed increases. She spins faster.

In a way, a whip does get its power from you, though not quite the way you think.

The power of a whip's crack comes from your belly, your "Chi" center which is your body's center of gravity. *You* are the mass behind your whip, because all the mass and movement of your body flows into the whip where the energy is focused.

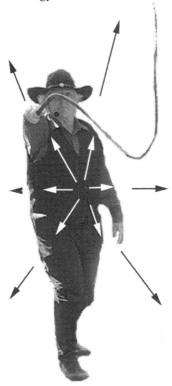

The real source of a whip's power

Use the mass of your **whole** body, not just the mass of the whip. Transfer this building power into your arm and hand, which will transfer it into the whip. Extend your arm fully to increase the purity of the trajectory and to keep the whip tight all the way into the end of the cracker. If you allow the whip to "fall asleep," the energy will dissipate before it gets to the crack. The correct form allows you to move slowly and precisely and still achieve the full power of the whip.

It's a matter of form, not force. You don't *make* the whip crack, you *let* it crack. You set it rolling, and then you guide it. As the cowboys say, "You ride the horse in the direction it is going."

You do not have to "muscle" the whip to make it crack. The power is already there as potential energy in the whip. You release it by using the correct form. So what does this mean to the whip cracker?

The speed and power of your throw, when it is in harmony with the natural speed of a particular whip, supercharges that mass into a force expressed by the whip.

The whip amplifies the energy of this moving mass, using the full trajectory to compound the energy with rising speed as the "rolling loop" travels along the thong. Your stance and movement determines the trajectory of the whip and whether there will be enough distance for that mass to compound into greater energy.

ANATOMY OF A WHIP

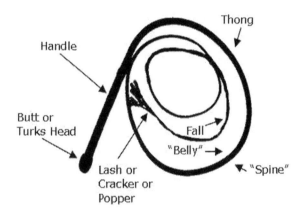

Butt or Turks Head
Knot at end of whip
Handle
Long-handled whips are called "Target Whips"
Thong
Braided length between handle and fall
Fall
Lace from thong to cracker. Easy to replace
Lash or Cracker or Popper
String on end of whip that makes noise.
"Belly" and "Spine"
Belly is inside curl of whip; Spine is outside curl. Whip wants to roll along this axis.

It's All About Newtonian Physics

Newton's Second Law of the conservation of Angular Momentum is a matter of centripetal force. Centripetal means "center seeking," and for something to travel in a circle, the direction of its velocity must be constantly changing. Any change in velocity, in magnitude of direction, means the object is accelerated. In the case of motion in a circle, this is called centripetal acceleration. The acceleration points toward the center of the circle. This is the basis of Newton's Second Law.

It's a vector differential equation: $Fnet=\dfrac{D(MV)}{DT}$ where F is the force vector, M is the mass of the body, V is the velocity vector, D is distance, and T is time.

As much as whip crackers, even scientists are prisoners of definitions, so let's distinguish "work" from "power." "Work" is the amount of energy you put into a whip, which is equal to the force you apply multiplied by the distance over which it is applied. This energy is converted into kinetic energy in the whip, and the formula for kinetic energy is "half the mass times the square of the velocity."

Newton's Second Law says this acceleration implies a force acting on the moving object, directed at the center of the circle. This force is called "centripetal force."

Power is the time rate of work (Power=work/time). Power is dependant on mass, and a high speed means a short time for the movement to yield high power. To restate Newton's Second Law in terms of acceleration, Acceleration=Force/Mass.

The muscles in your wrists or arms alone would be insufficient (without long arm motion) to generate the power necessary to get efficient acceleration to Mach 1. The power must be generated with the big muscles of the body, that is, the muscles in the torso and hips. It doesn't take much – the slight movement may result in a small velocity but the kinetic energy is large.

Andrew Conway describes it this way: "The kinetic energy you put into the whip travels down its length. As the whip tapers, there is less mass moving. Now, remember that formula for kinetic energy, half mass times the square of the velocity. If the energy is concentrated in one quarter of the mass, that means the velocity must be twice as great to make up for this. Now compare the weight of the handle and the thong with the weight of the popper. Maybe the ratio of weights is 1600 to 1. That means if you concentrate all that kinetic energy in the popper it must be moving about 40 times faster than the whip started out moving, and when you all that energy down in the last centimeter - CRACK - you are breaking the sound barrier."

Definitions

A single-tail whip is a flexible thong in which one end is thrown out to form a moving loop or sideways U-shaped curve and the other end is attached to a momentarily stationary point like a hand or handle. When the ever-diminishing loop reaches the end of the thong, the tip "cracks," making a snapping sound which is actually a small sonic boom — it may be small but it's still a sonic boom.

Every whip has essentially the same anatomy: a handle, a thong, a fall and a cracker. Yes, there are exceptions such as whips without falls and some people might argue that a snake whip does not have a handle, but even here an arm functions as a handle. The handle transfers the force of a throw into the thong, creating a loop which travels the length of the thong. As the loop moves away from the thrower, the loop becomes smaller, concentrating the whip's kinetic energy and making the thong accelerate until it breaks the sound barrier.

How to Identify Different Types of Whips

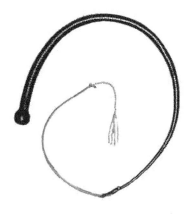

In the modern world, there are basically three types of single-tail whips: snake whips, stock whips and bullwhips. Whip cracking technique is only slightly different for each class of whip, as is the method of measuring it.

The **SNAKE WHIP** is a short whip with no rigid handle. It is flexible all the way to the butt. It is also called a shot whip or a black snake, and it's related to a dog whip or a signal whip.

Such whips are usually 3 or 4 feet long but some whip makers like New Zealand's Peter Jack routinely craft 14-foot snake whips of astonishing grace and accuracy. A snake whip can be rolled up to be stuffed into a pocket or a saddlebag. A snake whip is measured from the butt to the end of the thong; the fall and cracker are *not* included.

The Difference Between a Snake Whip and a Signal Whip

The difference is is simple - it's the way the cracker is attached to the whip.

The snake whip (left) has a fall with an easily removable cracker, just like a bullwhip.

A signal whip (right) has the cracker braided into the thong. There is no fall.

A snake whip's anatomy is similar to a bullwhip's except for its lacking a rigid handle, so you will see the same four elements: the butt/handle, the thong, the fall and the cracker. A signal whip has its cracker braided directly into the thong as a permanent extension. A whip handler can easily replace a cracker on a whip with a fall, but a signal whip's owner must seek out a whip maker to replace a deteriorating cracker. You can guess which one I recommend.

The **BULLWHIP** has a rigid handle 8 to 10 inches long. The thong arises from the handle in a gentle transition. A longer bullwhip handle 12- to 15-inches in length is commonly called a Target Handle, which why this whip is called a Target Whip.

A bullwhip is measured from the butt to the end of the

thong; the fall and cracker are *not* included in the measurement.

One arrogant TV actor/stuntman and his cronies keep trying to take credit for the longer-handled style of bullwhip by saying that whip makers everywhere call it "the (insert actor's name here) handle." This is little more than Hollywood hype, one of many ill-advised attempts to claim credit for something patently not one's own. Even the whip maker this particular actor credited with originating this laudatory expression expressed surprise when he was told. He immediately distanced himself from the lie.

What some Australians call a "bullwhip/ bullocky's whip" is a very long thong attached to a 10-foot pole. It is cracked by swinging it in the air like a flag.

Bullwhips are usually 4 feet to 20 feet long but novelty whips which double as hat bands may measure a mere 18 inches and they crack. At the other end of the spectrum, whip maker Krist King unveiled a 185-foot bullwhip a few years ago at a Wild West Arts Club convention in Las Vegas, and it cracked, too.

There are different types of bullwhips in addition to the Australian and Texan whips mentioned above. A swivel-handed bullwhip is supposed to be easier to spin over your head before you pull it back to create a crack. Frankly, it is sloppy. Any cowboy can sweep a whip around and cut it back to make a loud bang, hopefully without cutting off his ear. A swivel-handled whip is not required for someone to display such cavalier slackness.

I have rarely seen a swivel-handled bullwhip that had a swivel snug enough to not wobble even slightly. The whip falls asleep at the swivel between the handle and thong. This type of whip also rotates when it is being thrown forward, making it more difficult to keep on a straight line. The only advantage this whip has is that it's cheap, but a cheap whip is no bargain if you can't get past its built-in limitations.

Other variations on the bullwhip include single-tailed whips such as the French martinet, which has come to mean a driving, cruel perfectionist, and the knout, a heavy two-handed bullwhip with hooks braided into the thong and used in 19th Century Russia as a punishment whip reserved for the worst offenders. Being sentenced to a beating by a knout was the same as a death sentence.

The **STOCK WHIP**, favored in Australia, is a flexible thong attached by a knuckle to a rigid handle 16- to 24-inches long. Thong lengths range from 5 feet to 10 feet or longer. A stock whip is measured from the end of the thong to the knuckle which attaches it to the handle; the handle itself, the fall and the cracker are *not* included in the measurement. The stock whip's longer handle allows a person on horseback to crack the whip safely away from the animal. The 2001 Summer Olympics in Australia opened with the sound of a stock whip being cracked from horseback.

English stock whips usually had a crook or horn at the end with which a rider could unlatch a gate without getting off his horse.

Stock whips are the preferred instruments of Australian whip crackers who have named and described distinct cracks to the point that their national and local competitions have objective standards for scoring whip routines. The United States has yet to adopt an equivalent model, but there are some ongoing regional contests which purport to measure excellence.

The whole class of Coach Whips and Dressage Whips is

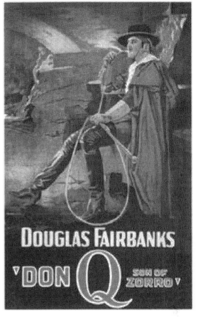

another situation altogether. These whips feature a long, flexible handle with a thin thong ending in a cracker. Because of the length of the handle, a fisherman's hand snap is usually sufficient to make it crack, but that's about all it can do. I have seen whip crackers able to target accurately with such whips.

Stage coach drivers in the Wild West in the 1800's were called "whips" and some of the more famous whips were Buffalo Bill Cody, Wyatt Earp and Wild Bill Hickock. Another famous whip, Charley Parkhurst, was discovered to be a woman after her death. These days, most whips are seen on ranches, circuses, rodeos, and movie sound stages.

Whip cracking allows one to safely and effortlessly exert authority over livestock. No cattle or sheep drover ever actually hits the animals with a whip because this would only bruise the meat or damage the hide or start a stampede of angry critters! But something exploding near them as loudly as a gunshot startles them enough to move away from the sound in the direction desired by their drover.

In Australia's Outback and in Southwest U.S. cattle country, the whip is still used as a working tool. A whip is used to urge an animal on as with teams of horses or sled dogs, but never to strike an animal.

Andrew Conway says that sled dog whips are deliberately made shorter to make sure mushers don't hit their canine charges accidentally or deliberately.

To recap, there are three kinds of single-tail whips: a **bullwhip** has a rigid handle; a **snake whip** lacks a handle; and a **stock whip** is a snake whip on a stick. The author here ducks to avoid being hit by a well-aimed boomerang!.

Belly Up to the Bar, Boys!

A good whip has a natural curve, a way it wants to hang. The whip wants to roll along this curl. This curl is caused by the bolster inside the

The inside curl of the whip is called The Belly.

whip, called the belly, so the resulting curve also is called the belly. The belly is the inside part of the curve. The outside of the curve is called "the spine." Belly – Spine.

It is your free choice to crack *with* the belly or *against* it. By this we mean should you crack in the direction of the whip's natural curve or against it? Some traditional whip crackers like rodeo artists are emphatic that one should always crack against the curve. To a degree they are right, because cracking this way increases the spring action of the whip resulting in a sharper, louder crack.

There are cowboys who swear on a stack of Bibles that you should never, ever crack with the belly. Some outspoken ones say this ruins a whip but I've spoken to many world-class whip makers from North America to Australia and New Zealand, and they all swear that cracking with the belly is no more damaging to a whip than cracking against it. It really does come down to your own preference.

Dante contemplates the "Belly Up / Belly Down" conundrum at Pierce College in Los Angeles

To crack against the belly, if you hold your arm out straight, the whip curls down. Make sure the curve is exactly opposite your thumb if you are using a target-handled bullwhip.

This way of holding the whip will make Circus Cracks more percussive but it makes simple Overhand Flicks more difficult, too.

One way to hold a whip: thumb up handle.

You can switch back and forth as the situation demands. There will be some cracks which will be more effective with the Cowboy-style "against the curve" style.

To crack **with** the belly, hold the whip so it droops down in front of you. Now, give the whip a half turn in your hand, so the whip arises from that V in your hand and curls back outside your forearm. If you move your arm back and forth, you will see the whip swing outside your arm, not striking it. Remember to keep the whip's handle parallel to your body.

Remember, too, that the whip wants to follow the handle, so be careful where you point the handle.

Cracking *with* the belly lets you to work *with* the whip. A move is more flowing, more graceful. It's the principle of "water flowing downhill." With this form, you can do more sensitive work, less percussive cracking. This is a relatively effortless crack, since the whip "wants" to roll along the line of its curve.

Align the belly of the whip outside your arm

Inside the Tracks, Outside the Tracks

To create "safe zones" where you will not hit yourself, visualize that you are standing in the middle of railroad tracks.

If you are inside the track and the whip is outside the track, you will not get hit in the head or the back.

If the whip comes inside the tracks – especially behind you – you will get whacked. And if a part of you such as an elbow extends outside the tracks, you will get whacked.

Inside the tracks, outside the tracks

To keep the whip outside the tracks, remember that the whip wants to go where the handle is pointing. Position the handle so it remains parallel to your body through the whole trajectory of its arc.

In other words, keep the whip outside the tracks as you stand inside them. If the trajectory of the whip does not cross the railroad track, it will not hit you.

When cracking over your head, hold your hand above the height of your head, not at eye level or lower.

A good whip *wants* to crack. It was made to crack, and the power is already within the whip, so your job is to aim and guide the whip, not to force it. The crack comes from form, not force. You'll do this by making the whip "lively," by giving the whip just enough oomph to energize it all the way from the handle to the cracker as you set up the stroke, not just when you crack the whip. If a whip "falls asleep" or drops or droops, it will likely strike you in the head, back or arms.

Remember that the tracks are on *both* sides of you. This is how I can make a continuous overhand throw that sweeps down on my left side and then back up into a backhand that sweeps back down on my right side.

After the whip cracks, it is ready to go again, so this can become a smooth and continuous multiple-crack move.

Holding Your Whip

With a bullwhip or snake whip, hold the whip so that the Turk's Head is in the center of your palm. Hold the handle firmly gently but firmly.

With a stock whip or longer-handled Target bullwhip, extend your thumb up along the handle. This allows you to use your thumb to aim the whip. It also allows you to know exactly where the whip is without having to look at it. Third, it lets you "pull the trigger" by adding a little extra oomph to a crack.

Put your thumb up the handle.

While you squeeze the handle of a bullwhip (or the butt of a snake whip) to pull the trigger, you press quickly and firmly with your thumb to pull the trigger on a stock whip or Target whip.

Some whip crackers prefer to not do this with a snake whip because the absence of a handle means you will place great torque on the whip. The whip's braiding will eventually weaken at this point.

Use a passive wrist, not an active wrist. The crack comes from your whole arm as an extension of your body. Pull the trigger to add that grace note of power to your crack. This wristless form prevents Carpal Tunnel Syndrome.

Ball & socket formed by palm and Turks Head

Signal whips should be held firmly and lightly, with the knob allowed to rotate freely in the hand like a ball-and-socket joint to minimize the bending stress in the thong near the knob.

This passive wrist approach also helps the whip. Since the whole arm flows with the whip, the likelihood of the whip's braiding failing at the point of continual and excessive bending forces is reduced.

Hand Position (Vee for Victory)

Notice the V formed by your thumb and index finger, with the whip arising out of your hand at the V's apex. Always crack the whip in the direction of that V in your hand, even underhand or sidearm. The flow of the whip comes from your full arm with a passive wrist.

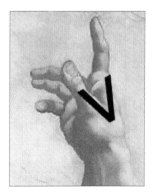

Align V with whip's belly

You can add a final fillip of power by using the Point and Squeeze technique (aka Pulling the Trigger), giving a quick, strong squeeze on the handle in the moment before the whip would crack anyway.

If I align the V formed by my thumb and forefinger to line up with the whip's belly, I can use that V to help me accurately line up my throw. If I move my arm and hand so the V is always on the imaginary line that I want the whip to follow, I know where the whip will go when I roll it out.

If I work with the whip vertically, I make sure the V of my hand is vertical. I move my forearm straight up and down, making sure my elbow stays on the vertical line. A common beginner's mistake is to flap the elbow out to the side.

Hand position #2: whip rising out of V's apex

If I execute a side shot, I turn my hand so the V is horizontal. I know the whip will travel down the center of the V if I throw along that line, if a throw is parallel to the ground. Keep in mind the drop from gravity that will occur toward the end of a sidearm crack.

If I perform a 45-degree overhand stroke, either forward or backward, I turn my hand so the V is also at a 45-degree angle. If you use a stock whip thumb-along-the-handle grip, the only change is that you'll use your thumb instead of the V of your hand to align the whip .

Practicing With Both Hands

With much practice, you have gotten good with your dominant hand. Now I tell you to put the whip in your other hand and try again.

When you try new throws with your off hand, you may feel awkward. You may be embarrassed or self conscious.

Don't be.

As humans, we learn more from our mistakes than we do from our victories. I hereby give you permission to make lots of mistakes, because that is how you will learn the most.

Don't shortchange yourself. A practice session is the right place to make mistakes – just don't forget to wear those safety glasses and that wide-brimmed hat!

Here are seven more great reasons to practice with both hands:

It will shorten your learning time because when you get tired with one hand, you can practice with your other hand.

When you use your dominant hand, you tend to think a lot. Intellectualizing can get in your way. When you use your off hand, you are more likely to not think and to focus on how it actually feels. You are more in reality and less likely to compare what's happening with how you think it "ought" to be. You get into the moment and into your body. You become a dancer, a child – in short, you become teachable.

Your dominant hand will learn from your weaker hand. After you've worked for a while with both hands, you may be amazed to see how much your dominant hand has learned from your recessive hand.

It is healthy and holistic. You are teaching both sides of your brain, making this an integrated experience. You will learn more completely by educating both the right brain and the left brain.

You will consciously see that you do things with your recessive hand that you do unthinkingly with your dominant hand out of habit. By doing something unusual and different, you see the whip's movement in actual reality. You won't compare a throw to some ideal whip form – which most throws never live up to. Use your off hand to get into the moment. Besides, by working both arms, you build up muscles equally on both sides. Proportion is beauty.

This method also alleviates the repetitive action which could result in Carpal Tunnel Syndrome or tennis elbow.

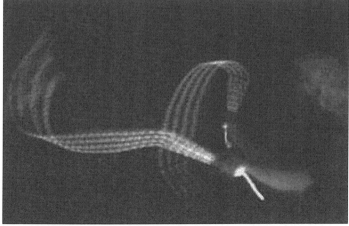

Blacklight whips easily show the sine wave form of a crack.

Cracking with your right and left hands is not the same as two-handed cracking. That is 'a hoss of a different hue,' as the cowboys say.

Working out at Will Rogers' Ranch near Santa Monica, CA.
This is where the Wild West Arts Club had its first meeting, years ago.

Ch. 2 – Let's Get Cracking!

The Three Basic Cracks – First: The Circus Crack – Second: The Overhand or The Flick – Third: The Stockman's Crack

The Three Basic Cracks

Good news! Almost every whip crack you see is a variation on one of three basic cracks: a Circus Crack, an Overhand Flick, or a Stockman's Crack. If you can get those three strokes down, you can do just about anything.

So check your clearance, line up the whip's belly, visualize the railroad tracks, take a deep breath and relax.

The Circus Crack

This is pretty much the simplest crack to learn.

Remember Newton's Second Law? If you increase any part of that equation, you increase the power of the result.

The Circus Crack doubles the distance the whip travels by going up, curling around in a S-shape without cracking and coming down into the crack.

This is the cutting stroke for slicing newspapers. It can also be used for putting out a candle, if you make the crack coincide with the candle's flame.

Practicing the Circus Crack

Lay the whip out on the ground in front or behind yourself. Pull the whip up into a circular arc like you're swinging a rock on a string. Give it enough oomph to get a good tug on the cracker. Make the whip stand out as straight from your hand as possible.

Use the upward swing of the whip to align your whip. Make the S higher than your head and draw the whip down in front of you on the same line you made going up. Bring the whip back down slightly under its original track and you will be on mark.

Extend your arm. Don't just use your wrist. Use shoulder rotation, like a steam train's drive wheel. Keep your elbow straight until your hand is extended over your head, pointing to about 10 o'clock. At the height of its trajectory, bend your elbow, pull your arm down and then straighten your elbow, which will extend your hand forward.

Bring your forearm down in a straight line as though you are cutting a chicken with a meat cleaver. If you've lined up the belly outside your arm and the handle is parallel to your body, the whip will flow forward outside your shoulder.

The idea is to form an S-shape in the air on the vertical plane. The whip will crack as it crosses over itself at the popper. The whip will crack close to you, from two-thirds to three-quarters of its length.

If you hear two cracks – one behind you followed by the one in front – you are "snatching" it forward and backward. The Circus Crack is not two cracks, one going back and the other going forward. It is one crack, one motion.

When you hear the whip crack, its energy is expended and the whip is ready to start afresh, even if it is still traveling with the momentum left over from the previous crack.

If you hear two cracks, you have expended energy behind you and you are trying to get the whip to crack with only half of its potential energy. You should hear a single crack. It's one stroke, not two.

So how do you do a Circus Crack? Imagine doing a wave at a baseball game. Yep, that's it…!

Exploring the Circus Crack - Tips

Crack the whip with the belly and against it. Hold the whip so the natural curve is coiling either up or down.

You'll see the accuracy is not affected but the force of the circus crack is greater when you crack against the belly. This method is also quicker for numerous consecutive cracks.

On the other hand, the whip unrolls more sensuously when you let it unroll it along its curve. When you throw with the curve, give the crack a little extra oomph by pulling the trigger with a quick, firm squeeze.

Make the motion slow and consistent. Don't rush the forward throw and snap the whip. There is no need. If your line is straight and the whip loops back over its self, it will crack all by itself. All you have to do is squeeze the handle to add the grace note that will supercharge your crack.

You can target fairly precisely with a circus crack, believe it or not. Do this by holding your hand almost motionless at the instant of the crack, aiming the handle like a wand at your target. You can aim high, aim directly to the front, or aim low.

After the whip cracks, 'ground' the whip to your whip side, or across your body outside the tracks.

You can train yourself to consistently crack vertically by putting two cardboard boxes on chairs and positioning them about two feet apart. Crack the whip down between the boxes. If your aim is off, you will hear the cracker touch the cardboard.

When you have improved to the point that you rarely hit the boxes, move the boxes closer. Keep doing this a little at a time until you're able to crack cleanly down into a gap of 2 or 3 inches.

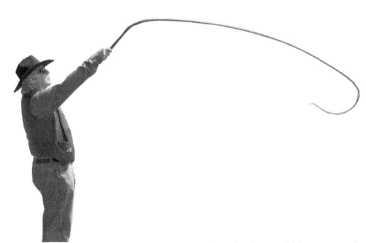

Crack the whip with the belly and against it. See which you prefer.

The Second Crack: The Overhand Flick

Set the whip in front of you. Turn your palm forward.

Pull the whip back behind you underhand, extending your arm fully straight out. Use enough force to lift the whip straight out into the air behind you. Use enough force to get the whip up. It should be at the top of its arc when you pause momentarily and then push it forward.

At this point, roll the whip on a straight line forward until it cracks. Do not sweep down in a circle before it cracks. If it doesn't have a chance to form a loop, it won't crack.

After the crack, guide the whip down outside the tracks.

The overhand crack is called the flick in Australia. It is like a capital D on its side, with the semicircle on bottom and the flat line on top. The whip handler stands at the center of D. Yes, this move drags the whip on the ground, so go gently.

Think of a swimmer: if you paddle only with your hands from your elbows in front of yourself, you will exert a lot of energy but not get very far. The effective swimmer reaches far back and sweeps far forward.

When you throw the whip, extend your arm fully. This gives the whip the distance it needs to pick up momentum.

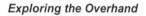

Be consistent and think in straight lines. If you pull the whip back in a straight line, you should throw the whip forward along precisely the same line.

If you pull back along one line but throw forward along another line, you change the direction of the whip and force the energy in the whip to dissipate. You might just as well take a pair of scissors and cut your whip in half because you are cutting the whip's efficiency in half.

Exploring the Overhand

The rhythm of the overhand crack is ONE-Two-THREE.

ONE is the low sweep backward as you lift the whip straight in the air behind you at shoulder level. TWO is the pause of the whip in the air behind you. THREE is the push forward.

Try to maintain a straight line with your body. The whip should be an extension of your arm. Just as a fencer holds his epee straight along the line of his arm, an accurate whip thrower keeps his or her arm straight, elbow in, holding the handle straight as it points toward the target.

The overhand crack is a targeting throw used to pop balloons or extinguish candles. I use it to slice playing cards and business cards. To be accurate with this throw, throw the whip forward at eye level so that you are sighting *down* the whip's handle.

Hold the whip in front, not out to the side. Keep the handle parallel to your body through the entire movement. If you try to stab a target with a sword by holding the blade way out to your side, you would be guessing that you could intersect your goal. But if you sight along the sword's blade, you're more likely to hit your mark. It's like aiming a pistol. If you minimize the parallax, that is, the difference between the gun sight and your eye, you will be more accurate. Be One with your target, Grasshopper!

Every crack starts with its set-up, even before the throw begins. You need to pull the whip in a straight line. If the whip is curled or coiled, it will try to straighten itself at the beginning of the throw and will likely slue off as the throw progresses. If this happens behind you, you will strike yourself in the head or on the back of the shoulder.

Variations on a Theme

The **UNDERHAND FORWARD CRACK** is the overhand crack riding from under. It's the same move made by a bowler.

The **UNDERHAND BACKWARD CRACK** starts with the whip set in front of you, on a straight line. Flick the whip at a spot behind you. You will need to put wrist into this crack, but the whip will crack behind you, rising upward after it cracks. Naturally, this works better with shorter whips, since long whips being dragged across grass lose a lot of their juice.

To perform a **SIDEARM CRACK**, throw the whip forward with your wrist pointing skyward. The whip passes by your body. The throw forward is a straight line parallel to the ground. It's like flipping a Frisbee sideways, underhanded. After the whips cracks, it will continue to your other side. Because you throw sideways, gravity has a greater effect and causes the line to drop as the whip travels. Experience will teach you how much to compensate so you can hit your target consistently and accurately with a sidearm crack.

Yes, the sidearm crack can be thrown as a backhand. Lift the whip into the air so it is parallel to the ground, extending straight behind your far shoulder. Your arm will cross your body, your wrist pointing down and your elbow parallel to the ground. Push your hand forward, not in a sweeping arc. Point the handle at your target or at an imaginary point in front of you. After it cracks, sweep your hand so the whip stays outside the railroad tracks.

Remember that with the Flick, you send the whip out to its full length. It cracks further away from you than a circus crack, which cracks half to three quarters of the whip's length away from you.

Remember: keep your palm facing forward so you know where the belly of the whip is.

Daring Tina holds a flower tightly between her teeth as Dante slices the stem with an Overhand Flick at an outdoor show.

Third Crack: The Cattleman's Crack

In a nutshell, the cattleman's crack, or the stockman's crack, is simply the circus crack on a horizontal plane instead of a vertical plane.

Where the circus crack is perpendicular to the ground, the stockman's crack is parallel to the ground. It could also be called an overhead reverse.

This is the crack most associated with Australians, ranchers and cowboys. The idea is to swing the whip in from the side so it circles over your head and cuts back in the shape of an S.

This stroke works better if you swing the whip in toward your body and then cut back so you sweep your hand outward, away from your chest to make the crack. Use your pectoral muscles!

This crack is associated with the notorious swivel-handled whip, which has little grace and less accuracy due to the wobble where handle meets thong. This lack of tightness results in a loss of energy when you throw the whip.

It also means your accuracy will be off. That wobble will communicate into the thong. You can't be certain where the belly of the whip is. I've heard people swear they have good swivel-handled whips, but I've never encountered one which couldn't be blasted into shame by a simple, everyday working bullwhip handled correctly.

First, make sure your hand stays above your head as you give the whip enough energy to travel in a flat path parallel to the ground. If you have the whip's belly aligned with your arm, the whip will fly around above and outside your arm (see the section on "Inside the Tracks, Outside the Tracks").

Second, make sure the trajectory of the whip does not intersect any part of your body. Hold the whip away from yourself. Reverse the whip back on precisely the same line you started with. If you don't, the whip will either hit you or flop out toward God knows where.

Do not rotate your wrist. This is not a wrist crack – use your whole arm from your shoulder to your elbow and forearm. See how slow you can go and still have enough energy to keep the whip in the air. If your form is correct, the whip will crack. You don't need to add a flip of your wrist. In fact, if you do, you will lose the loop's integrity. The form will collapse into a tangled mess. Just sweep your arm big and wide.

The easiest way to get the feel of this crack into your muscles is to approach it gradually.

Do a vertical circus crack, straight up and straight down. When you're comfortable and consistent with it, angle the whip slightly, about 30 degrees, and then cut it back on the same angle.

Extend your arm in a broad sweep with enough energy to make the whip stay lively before you cut it back. Keep your hand high, above your head. Have you remembered to wear safety goggles and wide-brimmed hat? I hope so!

When you can do that consistently, make the angle steeper, say 45 degrees up and back down. Keep increasing the angle as you get control of it until you are swinging the whip parallel to the ground. You'll figure out how much energy to use to keep it on a flat plane and away from your delicate face.

I suggest you use the V-in-hand technique to make sure you pull the whip back on the same line it went up.

You can use ground shadows to follow the whip is over your head. After a lot of practice, you will feel where the whip is, sense where it's traveling and where it's going. You will know it in your being because the whip will become an extension and expression of your body.

This crack will occur pretty close to you, of course. Go slowly and deliberately to get a clean, crisp crack that won't blow your eardrums as if someone had fired a howitzer next to your head. It takes no skill or knowledge or expertise to swing a whip wildly to make a God-awful bang – anyone can do that. But to be controlled, precise and deliberate in your cracking is the mark of someone who knows what they are doing.

The Australians developed their well-earned skill with stock whips because they needed a longer handled whip to hold out and away from the horses they rode.

It's easier to do this crack with a long-handled stock whip than with a bullwhip, so if you're using a short-handled bullwhip or snake whip, you've got to hold your hand away from your head to make sure the whip's line does not intersect with your eyes or ears.

Note From Dante: "I suggest you photocopy the following four pages. Carry them with you and refer to them when you practice. These four pages will help you establish a good foundation for whip cracking. This simple repertoire is the rich basis for a strong vocabulary in the language of whips. You will build on these for everything you do with a bullwhip."

QUICK RECAP – CHAPT. 1

Protect Your Eyes.

Where's the Belly of Your Whip?

Hold the Whip Correctly.

Visualize 'Railroad Tracks' (Safe Zones).

RECAP – CHAPT. 2

Three Basic Cracks:

> *Circus Crack*

> *Overhand Flick*

> *Cattleman's Crack*

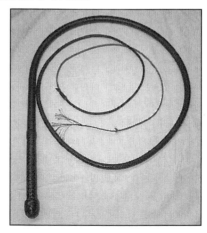

A well made whip is a work of art.

1
The Circus Crack

This is often the easiest crack to learn.

Swing the whip up into the air over your head. Feel the tug of the cracker.

While the whip is traveling backward over your shoulder, push the whip forward under the backward path. Your hand should make a little circle, like the drive arm of a train.

The whip will form an S-shape as it catches up with itself. The loop will roll forward.

Aim and squeeze. You can tell the whip where to crack.

TIPS:

Keep elbow in, forearm straight up, like a sword fighter. This keeps handle parallel to your body, and the whip follows the handle on a straight line.

Go Big and Slow — if you go big, you can go slow and not lose power. You will gain in accuracy and control. Use a lot of shoulder, a bit of elbow, and almost no wrist until the final "point and squeeze." Aim down your arm and handle. The whip will crack at 2/3 to 3/4 of its length., closer to you than other cracks.

2
The Overhand Crack

Use swimming motion, extend arm, to make this work.

Keep handle parallel to you. Swing whip up, higher than shoulder. Extend arm. Feel cracker tug all the way up.

Just as whip begins to stall, push forward, so whip travels over shoulder, heading slightly downhill.

Aim down handle at target. Point and squeeze handle just before whip cracks. Follow through to left or right.

TIPS:

The rhythm is 1-2-3, with slight pause at "2."

Keep palm facing forward all the way around motion.

"Whip Throwing" is a misnomer. It's really "whip pulling" and "whip pushing." Let the whip do the work.

Whip will crack at full length of whip, making this a good crack for accuracy at a specific point in space.

"Ride the Horse in the Direction It's Going."
Good whip crackers don't "muscle" their whips or force them to crack—They *guide* them and *let* them crack. Power is *already* in the whip.

3
The Cattleman's Crack

This is just a Circus Crack on a different plane.

Swing whip in wide circle, palm forward, hand higher than head. Give whip enough "oomph" to feel pull on cracker.

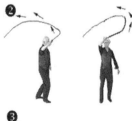

Bring arm forward so whip makes "S" shape. It goes forward along same line it traveled coming back.

Aim, point and squeeze handle. Follow through so whip does not come back at you.

TIPS:

Remember to bring whip back with hand higher than head, or you will wrap your neck.

Keep rolling loop tight against whip by bringing whip forward along the same line it traveled going back. If you change direction of whip, it will not have a chance to crack—it will "waffle."

Use pectoral muscles with big sweeping motion, not wrist, as if you are removing a big sombrero.

Make sure whip comes back outside your arm. You can "hide" under your extended arm, protecting yourself.

Ch. 3 – How To Pick The Right Whip
Marks of a Good Whip – "Two-Four-Sex-Eight, My 16-Plait Is Really Great!" – Short Whip or Long Whip? – The Key to Getting a Good Whip – Sure, Your New Whip is Stiff

---

Marks of a Good Whip

When you find a whip you consider buying, pick it up and examine it carefully even before you crack it.

Make sure the braid is tight. If the strands of the whip are loose, or if you feel a discrepancy anywhere in the whip's braiding, put it back on the table and move on.

If a whip is not braided tightly and uniformly, the kinetic energy put into the thong will dissipate at that point of looseness. This is where the whip will fall asleep.

Tina checks the fall of her whip

If you are not conscious of this, you will intuitively compensate by throwing your whip harder and faster. This will ruin your efficiency, reduce the whip's actual power, disfigure your grace and beauty as a whip cracker, wear you out quicker, and most certainly spoil your accuracy.

A crappy whip has newspaper, rope or other cheap filler for a core. One whip maker puts springs into the handles of his whips, making them more flexible.

The materials from which whips are made vary, but the preferred leather is kangaroo because the skin of that marsupial from Down Under is twice as strong as cow leather at only half the weight. This allows a whip maker to stretch the strands to get a tight, snug weave without breaking strands, resulting in a whip which is light and lively.

I have seen South African whips made from eland. I have cracked Mexican whips and Russian whips. I have seen whips made of chain mail. I have seen whips made of rope and rubber and nylon.

I have tied a cracker onto the tail of a novelty rubber rattlesnake and cracked it like a whip. They all cracked.

I have heard of whips made from hippo, elephant, walrus, and other animal skins, but at this writing, kangaroo is the preferred material of whip makers.

You can get a decent whip made of Indian-tanned cow leather or latigo, of course. This will make the whip less expensive, and if the whip maker is a skilled artisan, the whip could be comparable. There are some whip crackers who actually prefer these whips.

To choose the right whip, be clear on how you intend to use this whip. For example, if you are going to work cattle, you'll probably want to go with a stock whip. If you are interested in accuracy, you will likely want to get a target-handled bullwhip.

Consider the space you will use. If you're outdoors, you can choose a short or a long whip. If you are indoors, you might want a shorter whip. It's hard to crack a 12-foot bullwhip in a 14-foot room. Yes, it can be done as a bar-bet trick, but that's about all you can do.

"Two-Four-Six-Eight, My 16-Plait Whip is Really Great!"

When someone says they have a "16-plait whip," they're talking about how finely braided their whip is. A whip is made from leather laces braided together. A simple, crude whip may have as few as 4 strands in a round braid. An inexpensive, decent bullwhip can have 8 strands or plaits. A 12-plait whip is a sturdy, elegantly braided tool which can look beautiful and work superbly. A 16-plait whip is braided smoother, because it is made with smaller strands. It will also be slightly heavier than a 12-plait.

A 24-plait whip is expensive and requires a master whip maker's expertise to be made, but the smaller strands allow the whip maker to do fancy plaiting. For example, a whip maker can braid the whip owner's name into the whip, or weave flowers or other designs into the handle with different colored strands.

Some whips look like coral snakes while others have a purple and black two-tone look which is moody and sharp. I have seen pink whips. If you specify colors or combinations, you will increase the price of your whip.

The more finely braided a whip, the greater the likelihood that a strand could eventually break, requiring a repair job by the whip maker. Frankly, I like 12-plait and 16-plait whips, because the plaiting is fine enough to be consummate but rugged enough to be worked hard.

I have heard of 72-plait whips. Can you imagine a whip maker braiding 72 hair-like strands around and around, pulling them tight in order to make a whip which is a piece of art? A whip like this should be shown in a glass case, not used as a practical instrument.

Short Whip or Long Whip?

When someone says a shorter whip is "faster" than a longer whip, this is misleading. They both crack at the same velocity, breaking the sound barrier at 761 miles per hour. While one whip may achieve this speed in four feet, a longer whip may achieve this in 12 feet. So the 12-foot whip will have a longer hang time and the shorter whip will get to the crack point quicker. The acceleration to the speed of sound occurs over a shorter distance.

This is what we mean by "faster" – the whip's cycle is briefer.

Handling a shorter whip is easier than cracking a longer whip because it is lighter and faster. You won't wear yourself out as quickly during practice. Since it is "faster," you'll have to use a stricter form because there is less margin of error. Once you understand a crack and can perform it with consistency, you may then try it with a longer whip, for the weight of the longer whip and the extra hang time.

Working with a long whip is like doing bench presses with one arm. Learning new throws with a longer whip allows a whip handler to be sloppy. The poor form may become ingrained when a whip handler incorporates compensatory techniques which become bad habits. And that's not the fault of the whip maker.

Further, a short whip is more accurate simply because you're standing closer to your target. If your aim is off by a half-inch with a short whip, it will be a miss of 4 inches with a longer whip by the time the roll gets all the way to the cracker.

The Key to Getting a Good Whip

Know your whip maker.

Pay attention to his or her reputation. Good whip makers are known around the world. Every whip they make is a statement of the level of their craft, so if someone lets you try one of their whips, you can get an idea of what to expect from a particular whip maker.

Top whip makers in Australia are usually members of the Australian Plaiters and Whipmakers Association (APWA). While they do not judge the quality of members' products, they do monitor business practices to make sure they are ethical. They offer a newsletter, "The Australian Whipmaker," which gives results of whip braiding competitions around Australia.

There is also the Australian Whipcrackers and Plaiters Association (AWPA). Their newsletter is called "Get Cracking." Website is at http://www.australianwhipcracking.org. Send email to secretary Simon Martin (the whip maker) at secretary@australianwhipcracking.org.

A whip is very personal, so as a point of etiquette, never pick up anyone's whip unless they have given you permission. Think about it: how would you feel if you found someone sitting in your car, "just to see what it feels like"? Further, if someone does give you permission to crack their whip, don't try to see how loudly you can crack it.

If someone does this with one of my whips, I immediately take it out of their hands and chastise myself for being the fool who let an idiot potentially damage my whip. Hard cracking is stressful to the fall and popper. It also pisses off people within earshot.

Using the car analogy again, how would you feel if you let someone use your car and they immediately floored the accelerator and peeled out, smoking rubber up the street? Respect the whip and the whip owner. You don't need to shatter windows to see what a whip feels like.

You can buy dependably from a "name" whip maker over the phone or on the internet. But unless it's someone of the caliber of Mike Murphy, Peter Jack, Russell Schultz, Sharron Taylor, David Morgan, Joe Strain, Victor Tella or any of a number of other top-notch whip makers, be wary of buying sight unseen. A whip can look great in a photograph, but in your hand it may be dreadful. While a whip seller like Mark Allen can reliably tell you who made a whip, the fellow who is advertising on Ebay might misrepresent his whip, either knowingly or mistakenly. Don't look for bargains. A cheap whip is a cheap whip.

Brenda reflects on the whip field before her

Yes, even a great whip maker can have an off day. Perhaps he had a fight with his wife the day before, or he had a plumbing emergency in the middle of the night, or he drank too much coffee before sitting down to plait a precise and demanding whip. I believe that how a whip maker feels gets plaited into the whip. That's a reason why, in my opinion, a good whip maker is a living treasure in the manner that the Japanese government recognizes and respects traditional sword makers.

A good whip is like a good sword on many levels. It has a Chi , a life force which is palpable. The whip feels alive in your hand. You'll know it when you feel it.

Whenever you get a chance, pick up the whip you consider buying. One whip may be better than the next, even from the same whip maker. You may not be allowed to crack it, but you can move it to see how it responds.

Check the braiding. Make sure it is tight-tight-tight.

I've noticed that whip makers tend to make whips the way they themselves throw, so there is no one single pattern written in stone. Different whip crackers like different whip makers because they are more simpatico with that whip maker's style. It is not "one size fits all." Not by a long shot.

Different whips of the same type may have vastly different weights in their shot loading, the amount of weight added to the handle to increase the mass, which translates into a more powerful and percussive throw. Experience will show you your own preference. Some of my own whips have a heavier than normal shot load because this allows me to go slower and still get the power I want. This helps with target tricks, because I can make my throw more precise and guarantee that I will still be able to slice that banana, for example.

A general good-length bullwhip or stock whip is about 5 feet long. This lets you get the sailing "whip" experience of hang time, but it will be short enough to let you practice without burning yourself out.

Check prices. A store can mark up the price of a whip deplorably.

That's why I suggest that you deal directly with the whip maker. Most of them are accessible (except for the hard-to-reach, like Terry Jacka), and they love to talk to their clients. If it's a good match between you, you've not only found your whip maker, you've got a new friend.

You may have to stand in line behind the whip maker's other clients. If the whip is coming from overseas, it may run afoul of some patriotic bureaucrat wearing a Customs uniform who wishes to tag on some obscure tariff before you can collect your prize.

If you are nervous, go to a reputable reseller like Mark Allen or David Morgan. They are in business to make a profit so you will pay more, but you'll also be more certain of getting the whip you want. It's a trade off.

If you have something you especially want in a whip, a whip maker usually has no problem accommodating you, from customizing a whip's color scheme to tinkering with the weight of the shot loading, from varying the length of the fall to incorporating precisely the length of the handle you want. Don't be afraid to ask. After all, it is your whip, and if you get exactly what you want and you are delighted, you'll have made a whip maker very happy – and you'll have an instrument that you will keep and enjoy for many years.

Sure, Your New Whip is Stiff!

So are you when you get out of bed in the morning!

Your whip will break in as you use it, over time. There is no short cut which will not damage or weaken the whip. Some whips come to you from the whip maker with a shellac coating. This will naturally wear off with time.

There's no need to press, force, buckle or bend the whip back and forth to make it more pliable. As long as it unrolls as it is supposed to without losing any energy in the thong when you throw it, you're okay.

When you store your whip, coil it in the same direction as the belly. You can curl the fall around the loops of the whip to keep it handy, but don't tie the thong around itself. You will weaken the whip at that point. I lay my whips sideways on a shelf. Store your whips out of sunlight, away from air conditioning in a dry area.

A handle strap is sometimes braided into the handle of the whip. If you put this strap around your wrist, you risk being jerked off your feet if it tangles around something moving, especially if you are on horseback. It also gets in the way with volleys. Rather than let a handle flop around, I fold a strap and hold it in place with my hand.

As for conditioners, there are good companies such as Feibing and Pecard that offer tallow-beeswax mixtures that are great for whips and all leather products.

Condition your whip as needed. When it feels dry, rub conditioner into it. Let it sit, then clean it off with a rag. With only half of my tongue in my cheek, I tell you that the best conditioner for a whip is the sweat from your hands as you crack it. All the more reason to get out there and practice!

You do not have to condition the whole whip every time. The fall and the point of the thong may require conditioning more often than the handle. The more you condition a whip, the more you make it a dust magnet. Over conditioning a whip can also weaken strands. Not conditioning a whip often enough means the whip will be dry. It will not roll smoothly and the leather may crack and break, just like your own skin.

There is no conditioning calendar to follow. The condition of a whip is a result of how often and how vigorously it is used, the humidity, etc. The best thing to do is to let the whip itself tell you when it needs to be conditioned, and which parts.

Dante and Tina perform a dual bullwhip routine.

Ch. 4 – Techniques to Safely Improve Style
Setting the Whip – Point and Squeeze – Position Your Feet Smartly –
Go Slow – Hear What Your Whip Tells You –The 12 Principles

Setting the Whip

"Setting the Whip" is also called "Grounding the Whip" and it's a vital skill to have, for both safety and style.

It is a way to remove energy from a whip so that a crack that starts to lose its line will not harm anyone.

It is a way to line a whip up on the ground so the next crack starts clean and pure.

Setting the whip is done by simply flicking the handle to lay the whip out along the ground.

Setting the whip can be done standing or kneeling. Roll the whip out in front of you by planting the whip into the ground with enough force that it continues to roll out all the way to the cracker. Make sure the line is straight and that the whip does not slap onto the floor.

To practice this, roll it out forward, and then back, several times. Let the whip roll along its belly-spine axis under its own momentum. Do this with both your dominant hand and your recessive hand.

Pulling the Trigger (The Point and Squeeze Technique)

Point the whip handle and squeeze it quickly and firmly just before the whip cracks. That's all there is to it, but it's a powerful technique.

Let your hand hang there for an instant as the loop travels through the fall into the lash. The result is a crisp, sharp and powerful crack.

This is not "snapping your wrist" to make the whip crack. It's indicating to the whip precisely where you want it to crack.

Call it the "Point and Squeeze" technique, or "Pulling the Trigger."

You can execute this technique with a Circus Crack or Overhand Flick, or just about any other crack or combination of cracks (a combination of cracks is called a "flash" – we'll visit this shortly).

With this technique, you can momentarily pause a whip during a throw so you can get multiple cracks out of a single pass.

It also will make you more accurate, since you can now tell the whip the precise point where you want it to crack.

The Point and Squeeze technique is the single prime factor behind doing wraps safely with another person.

Want to do an arm wrap? Start with a stick first, then work up to a wrap around a well-clothed arm, just like Tina and Brenda here.

Tina holds a stick for Brenda to practice wraps.

In this case, Brenda does a circus crack at a stick Tina holds. Brenda points and squeezes at a spot slightly above the stick. After the whip cracks, Brenda holds her hand still, allowing the whip's fall to wrap around the stick from momentum.

If Brenda were to follow through with the crack without pausing at the squeeze point, the fall would slap the stick with enough force to knock it out of Tina's hand. If she did this during an arm wrap, the fall would strike the arm and start to accelerate again from the point of impact, resulting in a tourniquet action. The cracker would hit the skin with enough force to really sting and abrade.

Not following through is the key to doing an apparently dangerous stunt such as a finger wrap safely.

"Deadeye" Dante wraps Tina's daring digit!

This is relatively safe only because the power in the whip is expended at the point of the crack.

Because you supercharge the crack with the point and squeeze technique, it is a good practice to use when you pop a balloon. The only difference is that you make the point of detonation coincide with the surface of the balloon and not at a point several inches away, as you would with an arm or finger wrap.

_____

Position Your Feet Smartly

You tell the whip where to go, even when you don't realize it, because the whip takes every message you give it and tries to do exactly what it's been told.

A bullwhip is single minded. This is why you have to give it one message, not many conflicting messages.

Here's how it works:

The whip wants to follow the handle so you make sure the handle is straight. The handle should be an extension of your arm, so you make sure your elbow is along a line like a sword fighter.

More than that, your whole body communicates itself through your bones and muscles to tell the whip how and where to crack, and the whip picks up these messages from your body position and foot stance.

Correct foot position is either in line with your shoulders or with the foot on the whip side forward. Incorrect foot position means your body is torqued around – the foot opposite your whip hand is forward and you are so counterbalanced that you can gyre wildly forward and back. You wind up throwing the whip across your body from the

Foot on whip side is forward

side. Your body is going in different directions above and below your hips, and your accuracy is reduced to hoping your hand and eye will intersect on the target.

So the rule is, "Whip side, Foot side."

However, since an Executive exists to make intelligent exceptions to rules, you are allowed to make intelligent exceptions to the foot rule.

For example, if you want to look dramatic like Indiana Jones for a few moments, twist your body and step forward with the foot opposite your whip hand. You will look like a Marvel Comics character, even if you miss your target and strain your back.

How to Get the Most out of Practice Sessions

Warm up, practice, and then cool down. Stretch before and after. And remember to go slow.

Wyatt Earp said, "Fast is fine, but accuracy is forever." He was dead right.

Don't rush the whip. Every whip is like a sine wave. It will unroll at its own specific speed. You need to be patient enough to let the wave roll all the way to the end of the cracker. With a short whip, this will happen fairly quickly. With a longer whip, you will have a longer "hang time" in which the whip will pick up speed, resulting in a more powerful crack than a shorter whip.

The whip itself will tell you if you're rushing it. Listen to the crack. If you hear a thick, thuddy crack, the whip is trying to crack in the fall and not in the cracker. This is because you are muscling and rushing the whip, so slow down! When you hear a crisp, clean snap, you have allowed the whip to unroll all the way into the cracker.

You do not have to throw faster or put more power into the whip. The energy is already there. Let the whip do its job. Don't force it. Be effortless. There is actually more power this way.

So get the form of a throw or routine down first without cracks, softly and gently.

Break a new move down into bite-sized pieces. See how each bit works, then move to the next bit. When you put them all together, you'll get the continuous flow of a beautiful whip stroke, and you will be in complete control of the entire movement from beginning to end. This is the one best thing you can do to ensure your safety and the safety of those around you. Get the form down, not even worrying about the cracks. You can always add the crack later, but you can't compensate for sloppy form.

Be absolutely single-minded. Commit to each throw completely, making sure that every part of your body and every direction you point is on the line you want the whip to travel. If you are holding the handle out at a 45-degree angle or if your forearm is pointing out or if your elbow is sticking out, you are telling the whip you want it to go in those directions. The result is that you are giving the whip two messages, and it will try to do two things at once. It will flop or flip in the air, perhaps with disastrous results, but you can't blame the whip because it is only trying to do exactly what you told it to at the same time it is trying to achieve equilibrium.

If your whip is doing something strange or unexpected, check yourself first. If it is not the whip itself as the result of shoddy or uneven whip braiding, it is because you are sending the whip mixed messages. To get a handle on this, slow down, watch yourself closely to see where you are giving the contradictory directions to the whip.

Of course, rules were made to be broken (check the definition of Executive Decision in the last section). You can change directions deliberately to achieve a planned effect.

For example, in New Zealand some whip crackers play Tic-Tack-Toe by sending the whip forward toward a grid and rotating the handle slightly at the end of the crack, right or left. The result is that the popper makes a mark shaped like a C, a half-moon. Two of these facing each other make an O. The X's, of course, are relatively easy to make.

Hear What Your Whip is Telling You

You can help give yourself accurate feedback when you are learning to crack. Watch your shadow on the ground to see where the whip is in relation to your body, both from the side and straight on.

You can also give yourself good feedback by watching yourself in a plate glass window if you are practicing in a back yard. If you are in the ideal space, a carpeted studio or padded dojo, you may have the luxury of being able to watch yourself in walls of full-length mirrors.

Taking a video will help, but I do not think it is the best way. It can prove useful if you are studying it after the fact, like a boxer watching a past fight. But this is a function of analysis and not experience. The feedback is not immediate and tangible. It is mental. If you can remember what you were thinking while you watched yourself, it could be helpful.

If you decide to videotape yourself, make sure you can clearly see what you are doing with the whip. Don't crack a black whip in front of a bunch of dark tree branches and expect to be able to see where you're goofing up.

It will also help you to keep a whip cracking notebook, like a diary or log book, noting the results of each practice, what you worked on, and how you felt about it.

In addition to documenting your practices and thoughts, it will help you keep track of your progress. Over time, you will get a tangible report of your positive progress, which can be heartening if you have an off day.

And make sure you bring water to drink. Working with whips can be mighty thirsty work.

Twelve Principles

Throwing a whip gracefully, powerfully and efficiently is not merely a mechanical activity. Throwing a whip correctly requires clarity and clear purpose.

The trajectory of the whip is truth. It is as precise as a knife blade, as exact as a scalpel, narrow as a tightrope. As you hold one end in the air, a whip is a ribbon of road into the universe.

It is lightning brought to earth, divine fire placed in the hands of men. It is the speed of thought, the reach of possibility and the danger of dancing along death's icy brink. The area which lies within the arc of a whip is sacred space. What moves within is real; what lies without is a dream, a shimmering surface reflection.

Each crack is a jewel, a nova glint of star flash, that flare in the eye of one who loves profoundly, the gleam of the knife point flying toward the breathless magician's assistant waiting against the bullseye of the target.

Given all this, you'd better make sure your head is on straight when you pick up a whip. If you don't, it will quickly remind you that we live moment to moment in a world of logical consequences.

Here are 12 principles to help you become a better whip cracker:

1. Every day is different – and so are you. Warm up with the whip and check yourself to see where your head is. If you are tense, the whip will be tense. If you are angry, the whip will be angry. Your precision may vary slightly from day to day, as it will in any athletic activity or performing art. Forgive yourself for not being perfect every time. The goal is to raise the lower end of your performing zone, not just to expand the top end. Consistency is the mark of a champion.

2. Throwing a bullwhip is a whole-body dance, not just a snap of the wrist or a jerk of the elbow. As Yeats asked, "How can we tell the dancer from the dance?"

3. You can't get there before the whip does, so slow down! Don't rush or force your whip. A bullwhip wants to work in a straight line and it is always striving to achieve equilibrium. All you are doing is giving it permission to be itself. You will help your whip by not getting in its way, in any sense, or imposing your will on it inappropriately. Remember to ride the horse in the direction it's going.

4. Get in tune with your whip. A bullwhip will do exactly what you tell it to do and nothing else. If it tries to do two or three things at once and flops or skews or refuses to crack, check yourself. I guarantee if it isn't a shoddy or badly braided whip, it's because you are giving the whip multiple messages which contradict each other.

5. Develop your sense of humor. Don't take yourself so seriously. Give yourself permission to make mistakes. Fess up if you make a mistake, but be prepared to forgive yourself for making that mistake. Make your mistakes when you are practice, not when you perform with someone. Make your mistakes in practice sessions. Get your cracks down cold until you "own" them. Get to the point that each and every crack you throw is completely yours, not someone else's that you're trying to imitate.

6. Remember the Basics: Inside the Tracks/Outside the Tracks, Hand and Foot Position, Working with the Belly, Point and Squeeze and the Three Basic Cracks.

7. "Ride the horse in the direction it's going." After the whip cracks, it is immediately ready to go again even if it is still flying from momentum. The end of one stroke should be seen as the start of the next stroke. From the moment you pick up a whip to the second you put it down it is a continuum, and not a series of disconnected moments.

8. Do not EVER underestimate the danger of a misthrown whip. Control your environment, from ceiling fans to light switch strings to objects on the floor. Brushing against an object as you are laying your whip out will throw it off slightly, and when you throw the whip that discrepancy will be magnified.

If your whip is deflected by a half inch from touching something behind you, that half inch can turn into 12 inches by the time it reaches the cracker. That's bad news for any whip cracker, especially if you are working with an assistant. If something *can* screw up, it *will* screw up at some point, and it will most assuredly hurt you or someone else when it inevitably does. Expect this and plan for it by always giving yourself a safety margin.

9. Think Big. A whip magnifies motion and focuses energy. If you go big you can go slow, and that gives you more control. Give the whip a full chance to crack by using your whole arm, extending the whip to its full length to pick up momentum. I remind you that a good crack starts with a good layout and not with the throw itself. You can't compensate for a partial throw by snapping your wrist. Use a passive wrist. You'll add power by squeezing the handle to pull the trigger, supercharging the throw in the milliseconds before the crack.

10. Relax your butt. No kidding. This is a dancer's trick. When you relax your buttock muscles, you relax your whole body. Try it and see for yourself. Relax your derriere. **Keep breathing,** slowly and deeply. Don't think about anything except what you are doing.

This is where whip cracking is kin to the Japanese tea ceremony. In the tea ceremony, all conversation is limited to the tea and to the ceremony itself. Nothing else is allowed to be discussed. This prevention of extraneous distraction gets the tea drinker out of his or her ego and focuses on the moment, beautifully and calmly. Reality Is.

11. Always perform below your capability until you are well versed in a move or routine.

You have to "own" your routines and tricks, to make them yours by constant practice. Don't worry about making the whip crack in the beginning. Get the form down first. Move it out of your head and into your body, like a dancer or athlete. You can always add cracks later.

12. There is no such thing as "throwing a whip." This is a misnomer. It's all actually whip *pushing* and whip *pulling*. You guide the whip, you don't force it.

If you don't see the value of any of these principles right now, you will. For now, take what you can use. Come back to the rest later to see if they have changed, because this will show you that your own perspective has changed. It's a truism that you don't know what you don't know. The limits of your immediate understanding determine how much you understand something speaking to you from the future. Leave the doors open.

There is no short cut, but you will get there. You will move toward mastery of the whip if you pick the whip up and crack it with consciousness for a few minutes every day. This will get the whip into your mind more quickly and surely than if you cram an hour of practice into every Saturday.

If you want to add a metaphysical dimension to your whip cracking, consider sleeping with your whip under your pillow. The idea is to get in synch with the vibe of the whip Yes, this might be an athlete's superstition like wearing the same socks game after game, but I have done this and I still do it, and my whips and I are usually in tune with each other. You might want to use a washable pillow case, because the whip's dressing can stain sheets overnight. I use a towel I can reach under to feel the whip as I drop off to sleep.

Sweet dreams!

Remember to ask yourself, "Where's the belly?" and to turn the handle to align the whip's axis with the line of your throw

Ch. 5 – Maintaining Your Whip's Health

Making Your Own Crackers – Attaching Your Cracker – Caring For Your Whip – Your Handy Dandy Tool Box

---

Making Your Own Crackers

Your new whip probably came with some replacement crackers. A lot of whip makers sell additional crackers. These poppers or lashes can go for as high as $3 each, but you can easily make your own.

The advantage of this is that you can tailor your crackers for different purposes. You will have more direct control over how your whip functions, and since different people have different preferences, you can always be assured of getting exactly what you want.

Whips did not always have crackers, but the whips cracked, just the same. According to Andrew Conway, the Oxford English Dictionary says that the earliest reference in print to a "cracker" or "popper" was from the 19th Century.

The Oxford English Dictionary has some definitions and references which put the terms here into an historical perspective (I'd like to thank Andrew Conway for these references):

<u>Cracker:</u>

c. An attachment to the end of a whip-lash by which a cracking sound can be produced. *U.S.*, *Austral.* and *N.Z.*

1835 Monett in J. H. Ingraham *South-West* II. 288 To the end of the lash is attached a soft, dry, buckskin cracker. So soft is the cracker, that a person who has not the sleight of using the whip could scarcely hurt a child with it. **1880** A.A.Hayes *New Colorado* (1881) x. 140 Each wagoner must tie a brand-new cracker to the lash of his whip. **1890** R.Boldrewood *Col. Reformer* I. xviii. 110 Stockwhips garnished with resplendent crackers. **1907** W.H.Koebel *Return of Joe* 164 Fresh and efficient crackers swung continually at the ends of the stockwhips. **1966** J.Hackstoní *Father clears Out* 64 I'd plaited a whip specially for the occasion with a new green cracker on it.

Snapper:

e. *U.S.* A cracker on the end of a whip-lash. Also *fig.*, a sharp or caustic remark.

1817 J.Sansom *Sk. Lower Canada* 15 One had proposed to put *a snapper* on the driver's whip. **1841** *Knickerbocker* XVII. 277 All the whips were provided with red snappers. **1882** Pentecost *Out of Egypt* iii. 60 She brought out the last end of that question like the snapper on the end of a whip. **1890** O.W.Holmes *Over the Teacups* xii, If I had not put that snapper on the end of my whip-lash, I might have got off without the ill temper which my antithesis provoked. **1903** *N.Y. Even. Post* 29 Sept. 8/2 Senator Carmack is simply adding a snapper to the lash of his vigorous denunciation of the whole Philippine policy. **1949** B.A.Botkin *Treas. S. Folklore* i. v. 117 Showing off his prowess he first split a horsefly into pieces, and then tore a bumblebee into shreds with the snapper on the end of his whip.

Popper:

6. (The snapper on) a whip-lash. *U.S.*

1870 *Great Trans-Continental Tourist's Guide* (rev. ed.) 27/1 How often the sharp ring of the popper aroused the timid hare or graceful antelope? **1877** H.Ruede *Sod-House Days* (1937) 80 The lash is about l 1 / 2 inches thick at the handle, and tapers to the popper, and a good hand will make them crack like a pistol. **1934** *Amer. Ballads & Folk Songs* 375 And the stage-driver loves the popper of his whip. **1935** [see *bull-whip* (bull *n.*[1] 11)].

The cracker is the most expendable part of the whip. Crackers wear out or fly off their falls with amazing regularity. If you know how, you can quickly replace your own crackers without having to wait for new crackers to arrive from a whip maker.

Besides, making your own crackers is less expensive than buying them from someone else. It's no big deal, really. If you can tie your shoelaces, you can make your own crackers.

Experience will show you over time what kind of cracker you prefer for what purpose. The choices can be daunting, but nowhere is the pattern for an ideal cracker written in stone. It is your choice. Experiment!

Just as your whip itself should be braided tightly, the cracker should be twisted **as tightly as possible** in order to make sure the energy of a throw is fully carried all the way through the cracker and not lost in the jostling of loose strands in the last moment.

The **length** of the cracker also will now be in your control. A shorter popper is less likely to tangle on the fall than a longer popper. I use long poppers only to perform precision wraps with a cracker, such as wrapping a finger.

You also have control over the length and fuzziness of the fluffy end of the cracker. Thick fuzz will "parachute" against the air, slowing the cracker down. Slender lashes will be sharp and increase the cutting potential of your cracker, making it more like a knife blade.

You can tune your cracker, as Peter Jack says. By experimenting, I've found I get the best results by making my crackers' fuzzy ends a little longer than normal. I then separate the end fuzz into two distinct strands, snipping off one to half the length of the other. I then rub the end of the cracker between my fingers so the strands interlace. This two-lengths-in-one cracker gives me both the thick bang I want and the crisp, clear crack of the thinner strands at the same time. It creates a two-note chord with every crack.

While you're experimenting, don't overlook the obvious. Twine is a fabulous material with which to make crackers. It's cheap and easy to find.

Cracker Making: the Double Twist Method

Spool out a 3- or 4-foot length of thread over your lap. Without cutting the string from the spool, start back the other way so that you have two strands lying on your lap. Go back again, so that you have three strands. You can do this as many times as you want to. I vary the number of original strands from 6 to 12.

Move the strands together and pull them all tight from both ends, twisting them loosely together so you can pick them all up with a single pinch of your thumb and finger. Find the middle of the stands between your knees and pinch them together.

Drape the strands over a hook or nail at this center point and pull the ends taut. Holding both ends, twist them in the same direction between your fingers. As you tighten them, the strings will get tight and twisting will become more difficult.

As you twist the strands, rotate and lay the strands over each other in the opposite direction. For example, if you twist the individual strands clockwise, rotate the strands around each other counter-clockwise.

Keep the tension tight to snug the strands up. You will see the spiral of the growing cracker work its way down the string from the nail.

When you have a length you want, hold the strings tight from 3 to 6 inches and make a simple overhand knot to hold the spiral intact. I often use a double hitch. Snip the loose end about an inch and a half from the knot. This will be the part that fuzzes out to make the feathery end of the cracker. The more strands you use, the fuzzier it will be.

You want to make sure the cracker is braided tightly as possible. If it is loose, it will parachute in the air and flop. It will not carry the force of the crack all the way through the fall into the end of the cracker. You will wind up compensating by throwing harder and faster, unnecessarily.

Cracker Making: the Chopstick Method

This is my preferred method of making crackers. It is faster than the double twist method.

Lay out a 3- or 4-foot length of thread from a spool over your lap, 6 to 12 times. Don't worry about how skinny it looks because your finished cracker will be four times as thick as the combined thin strands now draped across your knees.

With a smooth chopstick, lift the strands up from the center of the lengths. Both halves will drape over the chopstick, like so:

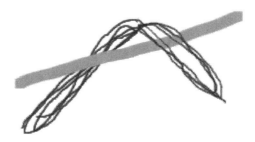

Put the chopstick between your knees so you can pull the strings tightly into a single thread looped around the chopstick. Spin the strings together in one direction. Keep going until the coiled thread is so tight you can't turn it one more time. Yes, you can use a power drill with a hook on the end.

I like to make a circle of spiraled string. Through the loops at both ends, I put one chop stick each, so I suppose this could be called the Two Chopstick Technique. This advantage is that I can spin one chopstick while the other remains stationary. It saves wear and tear on the finger joints and still gives me a nice tight braid.

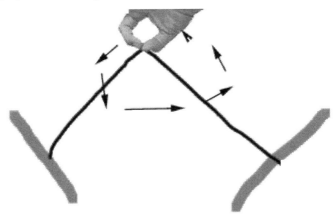

Pulling tightly with your right hand, pinch the taut string halfway down with your left hand. Pull outward. Take the right end with the loose strands and fold it back over the chopstick. The string is now doubled back on itself.

With the fingers of your left hand, give the coiled string a slight spin in the direction it already wants to travel and release it. The spring action of the twined string will cause the string to ravel together all the way up to the chopstick into a single thread, tightly coiled. Don't let go with your right hand. Hold the chopstick and the end of the string.

With your left hand, pull the sprung string out and tie a simple overhand knot about two inches from the chopstick. I also use a double hitch for this knot because it is smooth and does not make a knuckle in the string.

Release the loose string at the chopstick end without losing the spiraled string of the cracker. Snip the ends of the strings at the chopstick.

Knotting the Cracker

A simple overhand knot will secure the cracker. If you have OCD, you can tie each individual strand off, one at a time.

I like to make a double hitch, winding half of the cracker's end around the other half. This makes less of a noticeable knot before the feathery end but it does not interfere with accuracy, in my experience. It's your choice, of course.

Do it while you watch TV ("Knit One, Pearl Two...!").

Variations on a Cracker

While you are laying the strings out across your lap, you can spice up the result by doing a few things. Add some different colored string to the others. This will give you a multi-color, spiral patterned cracker.

Yes, you can lay a single length of fishing line down along with the other strands before you begin twisting. Avoid thick monofilament line, since you want a string that will remain coiled with the other strands. I like to use minnow angling line when I do this.

Poppers can be made of thread, fishing line, horse hair, kevlar, twine, silk, nylon, dental floss – just about anything that can be twined.

The material used to make a cracker can result in a big difference in the sound, both in volume and clarity. Cotton will be muffled compared to nylon, but you might want to make muffled crackers if you don't want to disturb your neighbors. Nylon is sharp. Silk is even sharper but the material has a short life. Hair from the tail of a horse is traditional and gives a clean snap. I've been very pleased with mason's twine. It comes in a variety of colors.

A fat cracker made from a soft string will thud more flatly than a skinny cracker, which cracks more sharply. It's your choice. Experiment!

Attaching Your Cracker

If you have a signal whip in which the cracker is braided into the end of the whip, you can skip this part. If you're like most other whip crackers, this is something you really need to know.

With a Texas-style fall, the process is simple: stick the end of the cracker through the slit in the end of the fall. Open the loop and push the loose end of the cracker through it. Pull the loop up and over the fall, then pull the loose end of the cracker snug. You now have a lark's head knot holding the cracker onto the fall, and it will not come off unless it breaks.

With Australian-style lace falls, you have two approaches:

Aussie Knot

Open the loop in the end of the cracker.

Stick the end of the fall through the loop.

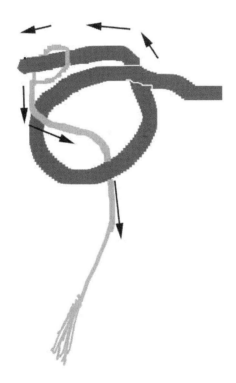

Curl the fall over itself without pushing the end through the loop.
Press the end of the cracker through the loop and start to snug it up.

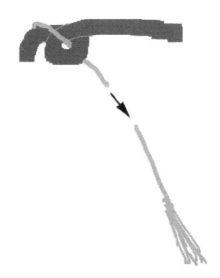

What you now have is a sheet bend-type knot which will tighten every time you crack the whip. The cracker will pull the fall against itself and should not work loose, but sometimes they do.

With practice, you will know how much of a nub to leave on your fall. You will want to make the nub as small as possible so the cracker does not touch it as it passes over the fall in circus cracks and volleys.

Dante's Favorite Knot

This is a good knot to use in order to make the fall-cracker transition straighter. First, attach the cracker by making the knot as diagrammed above. What you do next is straighten out the fall so the cracker makes a hitch around the straightened fall.

There is no large knuckle-like knot between the cracker and the fall, but you have to make sure the cracker is twisted tightly into the fall, really biting into it. It will still be fairly easy to remove, once you work it loose.

Now, roll the knot over the end of the cracker so it unknots itself. The cracker at the loop will now be tied twice around the fall, overlaying itself. As with the first knot, every time you crack the whip, the knot will bite tighter. The transition from fall to cracker will be straighter. Practice will tell you how close to the end to tie the cracker.

The downside is that the knot really does have to bite into the fall, possibly weakening the fall at that point, so with this knot it is more likely you will lose your cracker by blowing the end off your fall. But it's also easier to swap out crackers. It's a trade-off, so choose wisely!

Whip maker Victor Tella is one of the better American whip makers, and he likes to tie his crackers onto whips with a double-double hitch called a blood knot. Cool!

Caring For Your Whip

Take your whip out to a movie. Take it to dinner. Tell it how much you appreciate it. Buy it flowers.

I suppose this is what you'd do if you lived in New York City.

In the rest of the world, "Caring for your whip" is more the way you would care for your car. To keep your car in good running condition, you make sure it has gas and oil and water. You check air pressure in the tires. When you pull into a gas station, you take a squeegee and clean the windows, mirrors and headlights.

If this is too mundane, compare your whip to pistol. You'd clean the pistol, oil it and make sure it is not bumped or banged. You'd respect it as an instrument and as a weapon.

Should you do any less for your whip?

Watch where you're cracking. I suggest you crack your whip on grass, carpet or polished floor. Don't crack on sand, dirt or asphalt. Sidewalks and driveways are as bad as sandpaper on whips.

Try to keep your whip off the ground as much as possible. When you are cracking, only the fall and the cracker should touch the ground.

While this is not always possible, it's a good major tenet to hold close to your heart. Keeping your whip off the ground will not only keep your whip clean, it will save your finely braided thong from being subjected to ravages of abrasion and the cumulative damage of repeated impact with the ground. This lengthens the useful life of your whip and helps keep it in good working condition for the duration of its existence. If you take really good care of your whip, it just might outlive you!

Keep your whip clean. Try to crack so you are not continually dragging the whip through dirt. If you get pieces of grit or grains of sand in your whip, they work their way into the strands and act like tiny saws against the fibers every time you crack the whip and make the strands bend against other.

Clean your whip with a leather cleaner. Condition your whip with good conditioner. Do not use Neats Foot Oil or anything else which will give an oily, greasy coat to your whip. This will ultimately weaken your whip.

Condition your whip when it feels stiff and dry. The whip is made of leather which is like skin. When your own skin dries out from wind and sun, it can crack and flake. Your whip will do the same thing. A good conditioner is like a moisturizer. This is not harmful to a whip if it is used judiciously.

Over conditioning a whip will weaken the strands, loosen the braiding and make your whip a virtual vacuum cleaner for all the dirt, dust and shmutz in the world.

Condition your whip's fall more often than the thong to keep it supple and pliable. The fall was made to be replaced eventually without requiring the whole whip to be rebraided. You can condition it every few weeks or after every third or fourth practice session, if you wish. Judge by how the fall actually feels in your hand.

The whole whip will not require the same amount of conditioner. The thin part of the thong toward the cracker will need more conditioner than the thicker end toward the handle. The handle itself may not need conditioning at all. In fact, it will probably be better served by minimal conditioning.

There are no hard and fast rules, only principles which you must decide to apply or not.

Your Handy Dandy Tool Box

Keep a bag or cigar box with your whips. Make them inseparable. Here's what you'll find in my own sturdy but battered cigar box:

• string to make crackers

• chopsticks for twisting crackers

• paramedic scissors – they're inexpensive but they'll cut anything, even boots. Add to this a sharp knife.

• extra falls. Any whip maker has them, and they're only $3-$5.

• extra crackers, already braided. When you need a new one, you need it Now, not later. I like to use a spectacle case for my crackers.

• Band Aids, because accidents can happen.

• antibiotic ointment for when those accidents do happen.

• extra protective goggles if someone wants to join you or if you're giving lessons. Ear plugs for kids.

• needle nose pliers

• a dentist's pick is great for working those especially cantankerous knots out of your fall.

• a fid, which is a leatherworking tool like an awl. It's great for loosening up tight knots without injuring the leather. You can get it from a Tandy Leather Store in your area.

When folks are scampering around a whip cracking practice, it is usually these items they borrow from each other. One friend of mine always put an extra cigar in his cigar box, for a friend at the end of the day. If you've got your own tool box, you'll be able to handle just about anything in the course of a practice session.

Dual bullwhips against the sky at sunset – Poetry in motion at Shooters Roundup in Morristown, MN, between the chattering AK47's and the tanks . Long Live the Second Amendment!

Ch. 6 – Single Whip Routines & Flashes

Slow Figure 8's – The Cow & Calf; The Whoosh Bang; The Cross Up – The Snake Killer ; The Drum Roll – Flourishes – Pausing the Crack – The Coachman's Crack – Volleys – Flashes; Multiple Cracks with a Single Whip – Fast Figure 8's – Queensland Flash – Sydney Flash – Volleys – The Arrowhead – The Four Corners – The Fargo Flash – The Helicopter – Plane Variations

---

Working with a single whip is a great way to get a move down, first with one hand, then with the other, but double-handed cracking is not the same as being able to crack with both hands. It is much more complex and requires a lot more practice. It also requires that you are able to do a move with each hand before you can make the leap into performing with both hands at the same time.

There are some cracks which are more accessible with one hand, such as the Arrowhead or Self Wrap, than they are with two hands – which is not to say they can't be done with two hands, just that they're astronomically more difficult.

All these routines and flashes are based on your mastery of the three basic cracks. Everything is a variation on these cracks so you're not really learning new cracks, you're just learning new ways to do the cracks you know.

Slow Figure 8's

Start with a slow forward circus crack (Point 1). After it cracks, continue to swing the whip in a vertical circle rising behind you. Use the momentum of the forward crack to set up the reverse crack.

When the whip is overhead, pull the handle backward to form an S-shape behind you. Use your whole arm and not just your wrist. Make sure the whip's line is straight up and down beside you or the whip will hit you.

After it cracks, continue to swing the whip underhand into a rising vertical circle. The whip will crack behind you (Point 2). This is your setup for the next forward circus crack.

Repeat the sequence, forward, backward, forward, backward. This continuous combination is called Slow Figure 8's. These cracks are slow and lazy, so you have time to focus on the grace of the movement.

Tip: Point your palm in the direction the whip will roll forward and backward so the belly is lined up with the roll.

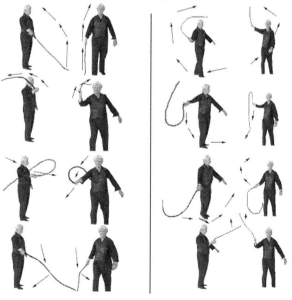

The Cow and the Calf; The Whoosh Bang; The Cross Up

This Australian crack is called the **Cow and Calf** because it is two cracks – one high for the tall cow and one low for the short calf.

Throw the whip in an Overhand Flick. After it cracks follow through so you are pulling the whip to a horizontal position behind you.

Here's the tricky part. Flip the whip forward with an underhand throw so it cracks as it rises. After it cracks, its momentum is the setup for the next overhand throw downward. Up and down, both cracks occur at the forward ends of the throws.

The **Whoosh Bang** is related to the Cow and Calf, except you start with the Calf first, bringing the whip up after it cracks to throw it back down into a circus crack. The Whoosh Bang is "the Calf and Cow"!

If you change the plane to a 45-degree angle over your head it is called **The Cross Up.**

Tip: Point your palm in the direction the whip will roll so the belly is aligned with the roll.

The Snake Killer; The Drum Roll

This one goes straight up and down with the whip making a single crack on the ground in front of you. Hence, it's name. The trick is not to whack the ground but to time the crack so it's only the popper which strikes earth.

And guess what? It's also called the **Drum Roll** when it is performed with two whips. It's easier with a stock whip than a bullwhip, but it can be done.

Flourishes

My late friend Brian Chic was particularly proud of his flourishes. He invented a self-wrap when he was 12 years ago and he lived long enough to see it be used by many other whip crackers without attribution. With a slight move of his hand, a whip would dance into a circle, sometimes cracking, sometimes not, but always creating a curlicue of grace and power in the air before he launched into his next sequence of moves.

Flourishes are nice because they are unexpected. They embody the principle of whip cracking which says a whip looping back on itself will crack when the popper reaches the speed of sound.

This is the principle behind how the great English whip cracker Vince Bruce cracks a 50-foot whip. He lays the whip out in a straight line, takes a running start and throws a huge loop in the air, rolling the whip along the ground. By the time the loop has rolled its full length, the popper comes up and cracks back at him, cutting a piece of paper he holds out to his side.

A fancy flourish is a great way to start a whip cracking routine. Lay the whip out in front of you on the ground. Pull the whip overhand into the air toward your hip so that you form a tight vertical circle beside you at waist height. Continue the trajectory underhand, forward and up. The whip will crack at your waist even as you line the rising whip up for your next crack.

You can do this same crack from the rear: lay the whip out straight behind you. Pull it forward overhand in the air so that you form a vertical, tight circle at waist height, and push the whip back descending straight toward the rear, over the line you'd set your whip up along. The whip will crack beside your hip as it changes direction and heads backward where it will crack again. Its trajectory now has it rising from the rear, and you are set up to perform new cracks.

Pausing the Crack

A curious thing happens when you pause a whip in mid-crack – when you pick up speed again, the whip cracks at the point of the pause. You wind up getting an extra crack in the arc before the final crack at the end. This is a variation on the Point and Squeeze technique.

Whenever a whip cracks it expends energy, but that is also the moment when it is set to begin your next crack. You can play with this.

Here's how you do a 3-crack circus crack. Perform the circus crack in the normal fashion. Instead of a One-Two-Three beat, perform it as a One-Two-Three-Four rhythm, with the pause at Point Two.

A normal circus crack is One-Two-Three, with Point One at 45 degrees in front, Point Two at 45 degrees behind your head, and Point Three straight ahead. The paused crack comes between Points Two and

Three. This adds an extra step so the whip hangs in the air momentarily without falling before resuming the stroke.

At the point of the pause, the whip will crack as it begins its acceleration anew. This will happen vertically, horizontally and all points in between.

Remember that the whip will start to fall slightly onto itself overhead before you pick up the motion. It will crack there. It will also likely crack at the back end of the trajectory before you crack it forward, resulting in three cracks. Do this continuously in staggered time with two whips and it sounds like galloping horses.

I have seen that I can add several such micro-pauses to make the whip sputter and pop up to six times along the arc of an ordinary circus crack. It's like John Brady's "Ocean Wave" but on the vertical plane.

Exploring How to Pause the Crack

With a shorter whip (a 3-foot snake whip, for example), you can perform this crack underhand going behind you, as well. Combine the two over and over and you'll get a syncopated galloping rhythm (clop-clop-clop-rest, clop-clop-clop-rest).

Perform this at an angle as a Stockman's Crack, and you'll get a Stockman's Crack with a little more sparkle and flash.

Combine this with Self Wrapping and you get a flashy crack thrown into an otherwise silent routine.

The danger which comes in a big way with this crack is that if you let it pause too much, you will likely hit your own hand. And this is a shot which smarts, for sure. You need to make sure the pause and pick-up maintain motion on same plane, or you will whack yourself.

As a variation on a theme, you can do side arms back and forth (Windshield Wipers) with a paused crack to create an interesting beat.

The Coachman's Crack

This variation on the paused crack is called the Coachman's Crack because Victorian coachmen used it to crack whips without startling or threatening to strike their horses.

The whip cracks behind you as it flies forward like a Tight Circle heading upward.

This is best performed with a 6-foot whip if you stand on the ground. I suppose if you were standing on something high or if you had a long-handled coach whip with a sheer drop-off beside you like a wagon or a carriage, you could use a much longer whip.

Practicing the Coachman's Crack

Begin a circus crack, but let the whip travel further behind your shoulder. Bend your arm extremely with your elbow pointing toward the sky. Make sure your elbow is straight in line with where you want to whip to travel. As the whip flies all the way down behind you, the cracker will "bounce" back up in front of you. At this point, quickly pivot the whip handle skyward to increase acceleration and the whip will crack right beside your ear (two words: ear plugs).

This crack can be performed with a signal whip, a bullwhip or a stock whip, but it is most easily executed with a stock whip because of the longer handle's greater ability to increase acceleration.

Tip: Mike Murphy's advice comes to mind here: he suggests that you keep your elbow low, and wait longer than you think is necessary. It works.

This one really requires you to be patient, to wait until the cracker rises up to the handle. It's not a bad idea to wear those earplugs because the crack will go off like a gunshot right beside your head.

This is a nice crack to perform behind your back as you face an audience. The whip coils around behind you like a snaking halo and the bang goes off right behind your head. Remember to point the handle upward and push sharply toward the sky when the cracker "bounces" and starts to rise.

This is a great way to end a show, if you are holding hands or embracing your assistant by the waist with your other hand. The crack goes off behind you both like a punctuation mark. The follow through is so big it commands the space around you.

The Hungarian Pig Drover's Crack

Andrew Conway can be credited for naming this paused crack, which was shown to him at the 1994 International Jugglers' Association annual festival in Burlington, Vermont. He learned the crack from a man who said he'd learned it from a Hungarian pig drover, hence the name – but it is certainly not limited to that use.

Swing the whip in a continuous circle on a flat plane over your head, counterclockwise if you're using your right hand. When the whip is out to your side, stop the motion of your handle and let the thong continue to move. After it lags for just a moment, speed your hand up to overtake the thong. You should see an S-shape in the thong. This will result in a pair of cracks as the whip picks up speed again.

Watch your hand with this one – that first crack is going to come at you, so make sure you move the handle onward firmly and quickly. Don't jerk it. The form is what makes the crack, not the force.

Flashes; Multiple Cracks with a Single Whip

A FLASH is a showy way to crack a whip. Some names derive from the area where the crack originated or from the use of the crack. For example, the Queensland Flash comes from Queensland (Australia). The Sydney Flash comes from – that's right!

In the Wild West, some stage coach drivers had a particular six-crack movement, one for each horse in a team, called the Wells Fargo Flash.

This approach assumes you have mastered the Three Basic Cracks (the Overhand Flick, the Circus Crack and the Stockman's Crack) and the ability to safely ground your whip.

You can't run before you can walk, so trying to do any of the following moves without having a good foundation in the basic cracks will only teach you sloppy technique and possibly put you in harm's way.

When trying new cracks, be sure to protect yourself from possible injury by wearing that wide-brimmed hat and those safety glasses.

Start slowly. Don't worry about the cracks. Get the form down first. You can always add the cracks later.

Here's where an experienced whip coach is an asset, helping you to experience what a good crack feels like.

Remember - if your form is correct, the whip will almost crack by itself. You do not need to muscle it to make it crack. If you do, it's a sure sign you are compensating for bad form.

Fast Figure 8'S

You learned that Slow Figure 8'S are basically forward circus cracks followed by reverse circus cracks. The cycle is slow.

FAST FIGURE 8's are more complicated. You will use your skill with the Overhand Flick and your ability to set your whip overhand backward with a flick of your wrist.

Throw the whip forward into a circus crack. After it cracks, "bounce" the cracker backward by your side, letting it pass by over the top of your hand. In other words, you throw the whip forward, and then set it behind you before it hits the ground. You will have a vertical crack forward which immediately rolls into a vertical crack behind you. There is no pause between the two cracks.

Fast Figure 8's are good to practice as a warm-up to Volleys.

Queensland Flash

If you've been practicing, you already know how to do this crack. It's just putting together what you know. The **Queensland Flash** is basically a Fast Figure 8 started with a circus crack and finished with a rising crack.

The downward trajectory of the whip as it comes back to crack behind you becomes the upward movement of the setup for the next circus crack.

If you want to make this a three-crack move, crack in front, crack behind, then crack again in front of yourself. You can do these all day and they are effective when performed with two hands.

Queensland Flash

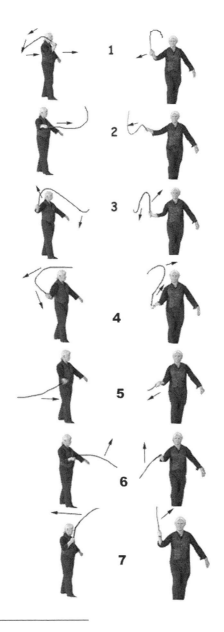

Sydney Flash

The **Sydney Flash** is the Queensland Flash with one difference: instead of starting with a circus crack forward, you throw an Overhand.

This one is more difficult to do continuously because your whip has to stop and change direction in order to execute the overhand throw forward for the next Sydney Flash.

Yes, you can perform Reverse Queensland Flashes and Sydney Flashes with the first crack occurring behind you.

Make sure you hold the handle upright – when people start a throw backward, they usually angle the whip's handle out at 45-degrees from their bodies, but this will make the whip gyre back at an awkward angle against the very trajectory you are trying to create. Remember: the crack starts in the setup, not just in the execution.

As with most activities, foreplay determines the quality of what follows.

Volleys

Now we're into the meat and potatoes of whip cracking!

A **Volley** is created by cracking the whip back and forth so every crack becomes the point of origination for the next crack.

There is no set number of cracks to qualify a continuous movement as a volley. In fact, a classic volley is really an extended series of overhand and backhand cracks.

You can perform volleys slowly or quickly on either side. When the volley becomes the basis for variations, those cracks have specific names, like the Arrowhead or the Windshield Wiper. For now, focus on doing pure and perfect volleys. Let's walk through it.

Traditional Front-Back Volley

Lay the whip out, either in front of you or behind you. It does not matter whether the first crack occurs in front or behind. A sequence becomes a volley basically with the second crack.

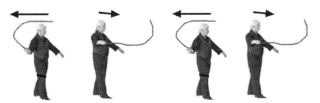

You can begin a volley with a circus crack or an Overhand Flick or any other crack in which the whip moves on a straight vertical line. The key is to keep the handle almost straight up and down – that's right, I said "*almost* straight."

You will need to angle the handle very slightly out so the thong will pass by your hand. If you angle it too much, the whip will be working against its belly and will skew in the air.

Crack forward, then back, then forward. Make it a three-crack sequence. After the third crack, draw your hand down into a circle which comes back up as you draw it behind you, ready to throw forward again into the next three-crack sequence.

Now, try the first crack behind you. Second crack is in front, third crack is behind. Draw the whip down into a circle rising in front of you. As it rises, continue the trajectory backward into the first crack of the next three-crack series.

Now try it with your other hand.

Side-to-Side Windshield Wiper Volley

With this crack, the handle accelerates the whip from crack to crack. If you want to do it quickly, make it more wristy. It's like waving a ping-pong paddle in front of you.

Once again, the key is to keep the handle *almost* straight. Angle the handle slightly out in order for the thong to pass by your hand.

Crack left, then right, then left again. Make it a three-crack sequence.

Now try it with your other hand.

Tip: Keep the whip moving.

Breaking down volley sequences like this into bite-size pieces allows you to practice the moves. When you get the three-crack sequence down, go for four cracks. Then go for five.

Tip: Use your whole arm in combination with your wrist. If you use only your wrists, you overtax your wrist muscles. You have more control over the line of your whip if you use some of your arm.

Tip: Aim for consistency. Each two-crack sequence should be a duplicate of the other two-crack sequences. When you string them together you can create very long volley sequences.

It is possible to crack a 6-foot whip nearly 300 times in a one-minute time period. If you are cracking with both hands, that's a hell of lot of thunder in one minute!

Remember to reach backward as well as forward or left and right. Give the whip a chance to fly. Reach!

You can do volleys on your left side with your right hand and vice versa. You don't have to be double-jointed to do this, either.

Variations on a Volley

Tip: I do variations when I execute volleys in performance. While the usual volley has all cracks occurring above your hand, sometimes I will throw in an underhand move. It is dramatic because it changes planes for a moment but does not alter the rhythmic snap-snap of the volley beat. You can move right back into overhand volleys without interruption.

When I throw an underhand move behind me, I keep the handle pointed downward after the crack behind me. I pull my elbow in tight to my side. I bob my body slightly to get out of the way of the whip. The whip flies behind my wrist going forward about waist height. Keep your palm facing the rear! You're going to be pulling the whip back in this direction a moment before you resume your overhand volleying.

Immediately after the whip cracks rising in front of you, lift your elbow up to get the leverage you'll need for the next move and to move your arm out of the way of the returning whip's trajectory. Crack the whip backward, After it cracks behind you, you are in position to resume volleys since the whip is already moving into that trajectory.

When I do an underhand move from the front, it is a little trickier. Essentially, you are doing an Overhand Flick forward into an Underhand Flick behind, back into a rising Underhand Flick forward. When it cracks at this point, you are already into the first crack of your overhand volleys again.

Because of awkward connecting angles of bones in your arm, you need to get that elbow out of the way when you pull the whip backward under your arm. Keep your palm pointing backward. Draw the whip to the front along the same line it had going into the crack.

When you draw the whip forward from the rear, make sure you're holding the whip's handle vertically, even though the butt of the handle is above the whip. Push way forward, so the whip extends all the way out to crack before resuming the overhand volleys in the normal fashion.

There, that wasn't so hard, was it? Oh, did I warn you to wear safety glasses and a wide-brimmed hat?

The Arrowhead

This is a very showy move, and it's fun to do. It's pretty close to rope twirling for a rodeo skill.

Another name for the Arrowhead could just as well be "The Changing Planes Volley." It's quite a bit easier to perform with a stock whip because the long handle allows you to pivot the plane more easily. With a bullwhip's shorter handle, you will have to exaggerate the crossover, really extending your arm across your body.

Let's give it a try.

Start with a classic volley on your right side. Don't rush it.

Tip: After the whip cracks behind you and you bring it forward again, aim at a point directly in front of you. This will be the point of the Arrowhead, and you will aim at this single point from either side.

Immediately after the whip cracks in front of you, flip the handle as you would when you set your whip and aim the whip to come by you on your left side. You'll need to pull a bit more with your arm to compensate for crossing your body. In effect, you are now executing a Reverse Overhand Flick on the side opposite your whip hand.

After the whip cracks behind you on the left side, flip the handle forward again and aim for that invisible point in front of you. The whip will crack again. Draw the whip back on your right side as you would in a regular volley and continue cracking.

Tip: You can work up to the Arrowhead by performing slow figure 8's, and then fast figure 8's alternating on which side of your body the whip cracks.

Doing the Arrowhead

Remember to keep the whip handle as vertical as you can. If you angle the handle when you cross your body, the whip will tangle around you. You want the lines of the whip's arcs to be perpendicular, whether on the left or right side.

Try to "bounce" the whip as you would do in a fast figure 8 or a Sydney Flash. The moment the whip cracks, the thong is still taut and you are set up to do your next move. You need to be firm but you do not need to force the whip. There is a difference, and the Arrowhead will definitely show you that distinction..

Don't completely follow through at the points of the Arrowhead. Aim and pause, give the whip a chance to crack on a straight line, preparing to reverse its direction.

Keep the whip on the vertical plane or it will hit you from behind.

From Dante's notebook: If you are a performer, you might want to try variations. If you mix it up through a regular volley, it looks like you're taking a wild ride, but you are still in control of the whip.

First, try making the point of the Arrowhead behind you. On the right side, as you bring the whip back in a regular volley, aim for a point directly behind you. Keep your whip hand high, because you will need to draw your arm over your head as the whip flies out behind you. You need to get that hand out onto the left side pretty quickly in order to bring the whip forward on your left side with a Backhand Overhand.

After the whip cracks in front of you, you can complete this come-from-behind stroke as you would a regular Arrowhead on your right side, immediately resuming your regular volleys.

The second way to do this is to start the Arrowhead the normal way. After the whip cracks in front, pull it to crack behind you on your left side. This is where the change occurs. When you flip the handle to pull the whip to your front, don't aim for the invisible point directly in front of you. Keep the line of the whip vertical and outside the tracks on your left side. After the whip cracks, flip the handle again to pull the whip back past you on the left side, again. In effect, you are performing a brief volley on your left side with your right hand. As the whip comes back on your left side to crack behind you, aim at a point directly behind you, right in the middle of those railroad tracks. This is the point of the Arrowhead behind you. Your arm will be right by your cheek and you'll need to lift your forearm quickly over your head to get your whip hand back on your right side before the whip loses tension.

At this point, you can forward crack on the right side and go directly into volleys on the right side.

Tip: Go slow, in the beginning. Form is all important, and you are working out a lot for what looks like a relatively simple move. It isn't so simple, but it can be done and done gracefully.

From Dante's notebook: I saw Mexican whip cracker Felix Lopez perform it at a Wild West Arts Club convention in Las Vegas, and the man epitomized grace and power - I could have sworn I was watching it in slow motion. This is a form worth striving for.

The Four Corners

Hassett's Four Corners is a Changing Planes Volley routine in the overhead plane which looks similar to an elevated Arrowhead.

A left-sided flat volley above your head is thrown as a backhand forward on the right side after the crack behind your head.

When it cracks in front, pull it back on the flat plane so it cracks behind you, then continue the move into a flat volley on your left side. There are two cracks in front, two behind, half on the right, half on the left. Keep your wrist aimed at the sky.

The Hassett's Four Corners (or "Four Pointer") is almost a Fast Helicopter. This crack is named after famed Australian whip cracker Dan Hassett who originated the crack. His son Charlie Hassett adapted it to two-handed whip cracking. The theory is that the whip cracks four times, once for each point of the compass.

Tip: You'll need a lot of wrist strength to get those four cracks off.

The Fargo Flash

Stagecoach drivers were once called "whips." In his book, Andrew Conway describes a particular flash used by stagecoach drivers for Wells Fargo & Co., which ran a cross-country route in 1858.

Twice a week, coaches left St. Louis for the 25-day, 2,757 mile trip which ended with arrival in San Francisco at a gallop.

Essentially, this is a series of continuous Arrowheads, up to 6 cracks - one for each horse in the team.

The Helicopter

The single-handed **Helicopter** will tax you to the max. Essentially, a Helicopter is a Coachman's Crack on the overhead plane.

Start with a horizontal Stockman's Crack. Before the whip cracks out toward your whip hand side, the thong will be moving backward over your head.

The trick is to pause the whip so it continues to move before you reverse the throw. If you do this correctly, the whip will crack behind you.

After this crack, you are traveling the other direction, and you will have to rotate the handle (and your hand) so you can perform the same stroke on the outside of your whip hand. The whip will be moving in a flat line above your head.

Tip: Make sure that you are doing this on a horizontal plane, parallel to the ground. Ideally, the planes for the right side and left side will be identical.

It's a little disconcerting at first to have the whip cracking behind you. You'll get used to it. Once mastered, this crack leads quite naturally into the next crack.

The Fast Helicopter

The Fast Helicopter is a left-and right-hand volley on the horizontal plane above your head, where it cracks at the front and back of each move on either side. You don't wait for the whip to follow through before you go into the corresponding crack from the other side.

Start off doing Helicopters, right side and left side, until you have a consistent rhythm going.

Now you will "bounce" the whip at the end of each crack and immediately reverse direction, alternating going to the inside of your wrist and to the outside of your wrist after the whip cracks behind you.

Remember to keep the wrist pointing toward the ceiling. This will help the whip stay on the plane as you alternate cracking on each side.

From Dante's notebook: I performed this move at a show in Minneapolis, and a few weeks later I wound up in hospital with sudden onset diabetes type 2. As a consequence of the disease, I was simultaneously hit with a case of "adhesive capsulitis" in my right shoulder. This condition is also called Frozen Shoulder, and I was unable to move my shoulder beyond a very limited range without a great deal of excruciating pain. I was unable to do Helicopters for about a year.

The Fast Helicopter is basically horizontal volleys where the Arrowhead is turned on its side and the V target (the point of the Arrowhead itself) is behind you instead of in front of you.

Tip: The key to this one is to keep that wrist pointed toward the sky. The whip will follow your hand position and you want that handle to be as horizontal as possible.

To keep the whip from hitting you in the head, angle the front crack down slightly. Imagine standing under a sloping roof, with the roof higher behind you than it is in front of you. Follow this plane so the loop of the whip rolls back toward you above the thong leading from your hand. If it comes back under the thong, you're going to whack yourself.

Be willing to really contort your body. There's more left and right twisting to this than appears to someone not doing it. You'll feel it in your spine. The crack feels odd at first because the bones of the human body aren't put together to allow this one to be a natural move. With practice it will become second nature and give you quite an enjoyable dance along with some fast, controlled cracking.

From Dante's notebook: Famed whip maker Mike Murphy performs the cleanest, snappiest Helicopter I have ever seen - two-handed!

Plane Variations

Most of the cracks named in this section can be performed on other planes where they sometimes pick up new names.

Plane variations can keep things interesting and make the best use of your space.

For example, as we noted above, when the Coachman's Crack is performed in the overhead plane, it gets a new name - the Helicopter.

Ch. 7 – Two-Handed Whip Cracking
Two-Handed Timing Terms – The Train – Windshield Wipers –
Florentines – Queensland Crossovers – Parting Shots

Being able to perform cracks with either hand is **not** the same as two-handed whip cracking.

It is more a matter of precise timing, because you have two whips flying and there is a danger of their tangling into each other.

Working with two whips will show you more clearly than anything else that good whip cracking is a matter of correct, effortless form more than it is the result of "muscling" a whip through its trajectory.

Practicing two-handed whip routines will wear you out a lot faster then working with one hand.

Two-handed whip work is more difficult and less forgiving than single-handed work. But the payoff, when you nail it, is tremendous.

Two-Handed Timing Terms

These terms originated in Australia, where two-handed sport cracking is the best in the world..

Together Timing means just that – you crack the whips at the same time, in the same direction, your left hand mirroring your right hand (or vice versa).

Staggered Timing means you let one whip lag just behind the other. This gives your two whips a syncopated beat, a snap-snap effect.

Balanced Timing means you work the whips in opposite timing to each other. For example, if you are performing balanced circus cracks, while you are coming down with one whip the other whip is rising. The sound of balanced cracking is snap-pause-snap-pause, with the whips alternating in their cracking.

Each Way Timing is when you crack the whips in opposite directions to each other. For example, if you perform circus cracks in Each Way timing, you crack forward with one hand and backward with the other in a Reverse Circus Crack.

You can combine Each Way movement with the three timing variations, so you'll get Together Each Way, Staggered Each Way, and Balanced Each Way (which is very dramatic).

Go too fast and you may call this the Which Way Timing!

The Train

The Train is a two-handed Cow and Calf.

We explored the single-handed Cow and Calf in the previous chapter. If you are doing two-handed Cows and Calves, you can get a sound effect like the accelerating of a train engine.

Perform the first cracks slowly in balanced time. This will give you an even, syncopated percussion rhythm. Now, start cracking faster.

As you pick up speed, start changing the beat to staggered time. This will sound like the clacking of the train's wheels on the rails. Go as fast as you safely can.

When you get tired, start slowing the train down. Drift back into balanced time until you pull into the next station and stop. Now drink a glass of lemonade.

Windshield Wipers

This is a fun one! You do slow volleys with two whips traveling left at the same time, right at the same time. One whip will be in front as the other passes your body, alternating back and forth. The result is that they do not cross each other.

It's easier to do this with stock whips, of course, because all the action can be in your wrists (that is, the handles).

Irish Windshield Wipers

Do the basic Windshield Wipers (or Windscreen Wipers, as they are called in Australia). You'll move the whips in the same direction at the same time and they'll avoid each other pretty completely.

Now perform the same move in opposite directions so both whips go forward and backward at the same time. The whips will cross in front, so a slightly staggered timing and different angle of attack for each whip will allow you to do this without tangling your whips.

Florentines

These are two-handed Overhand Cracks which cross in front of you and come back around the opposite shoulders. You'll make the following cracks backhands which end by coming around your shoulders on the whip-hand sides.

Make sure you keep the whip handles straight and the planes of the whips as vertical as possible. You want the whips to crack coming down. If you make a sidearm shot out of an Overhand Crack, you will not be lined up straight to do the follow-up throw to the other side.

The hand that leads, that is, the hand that goes above the other one, is called the **Lead Hand.**

You can add a little fillip here by changing the Lead hand by crossing one arm under the other but keeping the whip on the same side of your body. The arm on the top side is going to have more room to maneuver than the lower arm, so make that the arm you circle to come back on the underside of the your other arm. To get back into regular timing, lead with this arm again to "untie" the crossed arms.

Throw your right hand forward in an Overhand Flick as you lift your left-hand whip to throw forward. As you follow through down to your left side with the right-hand whip, throw your left-hand whip forward with your left hand over your right hand. The left-hand whip will follow through on your right side, and you will lift it into an arc behind you as you throw the right-hand whip forward from your left side. It will follow through on your right side. As it does this, throw your left-hand whip forward from your right side and use the follow through past your left side to line the left-hand whip up for the next forward throw from the left side.

From Dante's notebook: In my notes, I refer to this move as "Swashbucklers" because it is so descriptive of the move. We first tried doing this with two and four whips for a pirate sword fight sequence with black light whips at a sci-fi convention.

Queensland Crossover

With this one, execute Slow Figure 8's on the overhead plane with both hands. It looks similar to John Brady's Under the Southern Cross. We can vary the timing, but this is, essentially, two-handed Helicopters. There is almost no "down" to this – it is as horizontal as you can make it.

From Dante's notebook: I heard John Brady call it the Queensland Cross. He said it is also called the Southern Cross.

When he came to the U.S. in 1968, he renamed his version the Stars and Stripes Forever because it matched that song's rhythm.

There are more cracks to discover, of course, but most will be variations on themes you already know. For example, the Drum Roll is basically a two-handed Snake Killer performed in Balanced Time.

When you see a new crack that catches your breath, know that you can approach it, armed with the expertise you already have.

Tip: Break a new crack into its components, remembering to start slowly. Get the form right and worry about putting in the cracks later.

Some cracks are downright nasty for the level of expertise they require, like the notorious Kahona. I won't even begin to describe its sequence of changing planes beyond suggesting that you get a copy of Mike Murphy's videotape. In this case, one show is worth ten thousand words.

Brenda executes a superb Cattleman's Crack!

Ch. 8 – Some Basic Tricks

Tips on Equipment for Tricks – Remember Safety – Half Dozen Self Cutting Tricks – Playing Cards – Snuffing Candles – Slicing a Banana – Newspaper – Wraps and Grabs – Styrofoam Cutting Variations – Coin Off Tongue – Flying Streamer Cut Stunt – The Rose Show

---

The basic tricks which can be done with a bullwhip involve cracking, targeting and wrapping, with each trick requiring a different degree of accuracy for safety and dramatic effect.

We'll look first at tricks which can be performed alone, then at tricks in which the whip handler has someone holding objects for them.

Please understand I am not telling you how YOU should do it. I am only telling you how I do it. The key is to make each trick your own. In short, don't perform my tricks – perform YOUR tricks. Make this your own journey. As Andrew Conway says, "Think of it as a pilgrimage – the important thing is not being there, it is going there."

Yes, I refer to an assistant as "she." No sexism is intended. Female whip crackers can use male assistants and people of the same gender can assist each other in whip acts, as well. Oh, the poverty of the English language...!

Tips on Equipment for Tricks

The best material with which to performing cutting tricks is **styrofoam strips**, thinly sliced from the plates used by grocery store meat departments. They are light, they break easily where they are hit, and they are inexpensive, if not free. They are also easier to see from a distance than sticks of spaghetti or some other skinny targets. Styrofoam strips can be colored with glow-in-the-dark spray paint if you are doing a blacklight show.

Balloons can be problematic. Some seem to be as strong as condoms. Avoid balloons advertised as being good for helium – this latex is thicker, denser and harder to pop. Even water-bomb balloons can be pop-resistant, although they are made to break. These balloons are supposed to explode at the slightest touch.

The key is to inflate a balloon to the point of bursting. If the skin of the balloon is slightly soft, it will absorb the blow and not pop. Strike with cracker. The threads will slash the skin of the balloon.

A balloon pop stunt begins with Dante & Tina.

If you hit with the knot in the cracker, you have to really whack it. Crack the whip just as the cracker touches the balloon – if the whip cracks before it hits the balloon, you will simply wallop the balloon and may not pop it.

If you are using an assistant, have them hold the balloon tightly and rigidly. If it flops around, it will absorb the blow and not pop. If it is held firmly to resist the crack, it will pop. If you are using a volunteer, remember to give them safety glasses – you never know where the pieces of the erupted balloon will fly!

I have explored various cutting "cheats" added into a cracker, from fish hooks to paper clips twined through the cracker above the knot like a twist of barbed wire. I determined this was dangerous to me, to the audience and to my assistant. The most consistent way to guarantee success is to do the trick the right way. It's also the safest way.

Bang! The balloon explodes the instant the whip cracks!

Cheating also limited the use of the whip to that single trick. I didn't want to be doing wraps, for example, with a whip which would cut like a Russian knout if I was slightly off. The addition of a gimmick like this also impeded the smooth flow of the cracker and made the crack less likely to be achieved consistently. I will not even mention the danger of a barb flying off the cracker toward an observer. I discontinued the practice. There is no shortcut to this one. You have to actually do it.

To make the balloon pop more dramatic, I often stuff the balloon with multi-color feathers. If you use talcum powder, the fine dust gets on everything, and it is slippery on a wooden stage.   If you fill it with cigar smoke, it's politically incorrect in this anti-smoking world – but it does look good.

Playing cards are *not* all the same. Bicycle Playing Cards and other cards which are "coated" slice cleanly. Simple pasteboard cards may slice, maybe not. A playing card is about as small as you can get with a hand-held object which can be seen by people in the balcony.

Remember Safety – You Do Not Get a Second Chance

If you cut a cigarette from your own mouth or someone else's mouth, the cigarette will more than likely explode and shower little flecks of tobacco and ash everywhere – including into the eyes of anyone standing close by. I strongly suggest you use a styrofoam, strip, instead.

If you are a professional performer, it is also not a good idea to show cigarettes in a fun context, especially if you are performing for children or families. Relegate cigarettes to the tricks of yesteryear – in this age of animal-less circuses, using cigarettes in your stunt dates you as a throwback to the 1940s.

If you put talcum powder or confetti inside a balloon so the audience can see the explosion more clearly, remember that this atomized material has to go somewhere – all over the stage. This potentially slippery material will be under the feet of the performer following you. It will also litter the stage unless you are cleaning as you go.

It breaks the feel of a performance for the audience to see the artists suddenly bend over and start picking up garbage before they scamper offstage with shreds of paper in their hands.

With candles, remember that if you crack near or close to melting wax, you may splash it, usually in a straight line extending from you through the candle to the audience or assistant on the other side.

Bear all this in mind when you are blocking out your tricks, both alone and with an assistant.

Half a Dozen Self Cutting Tricks

If you get good at this, you can slice a single strip of styrofoam a number of times before you have to reach for a fresh one. There are more than merely six ways to cut styrofoam strips which you hold for yourself, but these are just to get you started. Feel free to experiment.

The principle here is simple: remember the Railroad Tracks. If the whip is traveling in a single plane, any object crossing that plane as the whip passes will be hit. If it is a strip of styrofoam, it will break at that point.

A lot of these cuts do not rely on the cracker cutting the styrofoam strip. The fall, or even the thong, may break the styrofoam. The effect is still dramatic if you get a good crack at the end. Some folks in the audience may believe they are simultaneous, but even if they don't, it can still be a thrilling, effective display of precision and daring.

First Cut: hold styrofoam strip between fingers of whip hand so the strip extends out, parallel to the floor. Do a simple circus crack. As the whip passes by your hand, it will strike the strip and break it. The crack follows almost immediately, adding to the effect.

Second Cut: Hold styrofoam strip behind your back at hip level, extending past your shoulder. You can now perform a circus crack so the tip of the whip will pass through the styrofoam strip behind you before you crack it forward.

Third Cut: Hold styrofoam strip behind your head at ear level so the strip extends out past your shoulder. Do a circus crack and as the whip passes over your shoulder going forward, it will break the styrofoam strip.

Fourth Cut: Stick the styrofoam through the fingers of your off hand so you can place your hand flat on your head. The styrofoam strip should stick straight up from your skull like a radio antenna. Perform a Helicopter or Stockman's Crack over your head. The back of your hand will protect your head if you curl your fingers slightly down into your skull. The strip will be cut as the whip passes through it.

Fifth Cut: Put your hand behind your back so the styrofoam strip extends out under your arm, close to your body. Send the whip forward with an underhand, rising crack and pull it back quickly, following through. The whip will cut the styrofoam under your arm pit. The danger here is that the whip is cracking as it comes back toward you. Be careful.

Sixth Cut: Hold the styrofoam strip with your left hand extended so it points forward, about waist high. Using a longer whip, line the whip up on the floor at about a 30-degree angle forward on the floor.

Use the handle and draw a short, tight circle quickly in the air about 6 inches away from the strip. Follow through to extend your arm fully out to your right side, away from your body. The whip will follow the trajectory you have drawn in the air, and as it passes by the point of its smallest diameter (right at the object), it will crack and slice the styrofoam strip. Wear a glove while you're practicing this one. It might not seem like it, but you will get the same forceful whack as if someone had taken deliberate aim at you from 6 feet away. The advantage of this particular trick is that you can do a self cut with a long whip in a narrow, tight space. I've used an 8-foot whip on a 10-foot stage for this trick.

Tip: Pay attention to the actual path of the whip. Make sure the whip connects with the strip at right angles, on the thinnest edge of the strip's surface. This makes the cutting cleaner.

Playing Cards

Playing cards are fun to cut. The key is to chock the card so it does not bend as it absorbs the blow.

Have the assistant show the card to the audience, white side out. Let the audience see the pips or the figure on the card.

The assistant should stand with the card in her right hand, looking over her right shoulder at you. The advantage of this position for all holding tricks is that the arm acts as a shield for the front of the body and face should the air conditioning come on to blow the whip in her direction.

The card needs to be held tightly at the upper corner, horizontally, with the short side butted against the closed fingers of the same hand. This is to create a firm, unyielding edge. Otherwise, you may cut halfway through the card and send the remnant flying out of your holder's hand. Not classy.

Make sure the holder understands that you cannot see behind the card, so her thumb gripping the back of the card should not extend past her finger on the front. If you make sure you are not hitting the finger, you can assume you are not going to strike the thumb, either.

The assistant should hold the card with the white face toward you. This makes the card easier to see in the varying light conditions of different performances.

Crack outside for distance. Then move in toward the card. You should get to the point you can predictably get to the edge of the card with two or three cracks.

Don't target the middle of the card. Remember that the holder's hand is taking up a portion of the card, so what looks like the center of the card is actually closer to the fingers than the real center line of your target.

After the card is cut, your assistant should hold the card up with the white side toward the audience. They can clearly see there is a slice missing from the card, pips missing the original count. If the assistant holds up the back of the card, the mosaic style of the back of the card will make seeing the trick's success more difficult for the audience.

If the cut piece falls at her feet, it is appropriate to pick both pieces up to show to the audience, one piece in each hand. This dramatizes the actual slice.

Understand that when the audience applauds, it is not only clapping for your expertise – it is honoring the amazing bravery of your assistant, as well. Acknowledge your assistant – the audience will love you all the more for it. Your assistant deserves this accolade, anyway.

For this trick, I sometimes pull the playing card out of my pocket and show it to the audience myself. I walk over to my assistant and place the card not in her hand, but in between her teeth. As I turn my back and walk back to my spot, my assistant plays with the audience's fears by staring wide-eyed at the card under her nose, then shaking her head emphatically and taking the card out of her mouth, to hold it in her hand – which is what we'd planned in the first place. This heightens the anxiety of the audience and then gives them a moment of comedy relief before the dangerous work resumes for real.

The great Vince Bruce showed that it is possible to cut cards as they are flipped into the air. I used to do this, until I saw that a card could be hit in such a way that it would fly into the audience. As some sideshow performers have demonstrated, a playing card spinning at a high speed can cut just as surely as a knife. I discontinued doing these stunts in my public routines but I still enjoy the challenge in my private practice sessions!

Use the right cards. I recommend Bicycle Playing Cards – they are consistent, firm, coated, and they slice superbly.

The key to this trick is cracking consistently at the same spot in the air, and throwing the playing cards predictably into that spot. First, get the elements down, and then put the elements together.

First practice tossing the cards without the whip.

Use a magician's card toss technique to give the card a hellacious spin. Extend one finger down the long side of the card. Cock your wrist as you pull your arm back. Throw with your hand, uncocking your wrist so you make the card spin as much as you can without actually sending it sailing across the room. This makes it hang in the air and spin more precisely. Try to toss the card so it is spins vertically in front of you – this makes it easier to target. Practice until you can toss the cards so they cross the same point in the air in front of you at the same speed, almost every time. When you get this down, put the cards down and pick up your whip (we'll come back to the cards shortly).

Start with a shorter whip. Do circus cracks over and over, cracking the whip at exactly the same point in space in front of you. Start moving your other hand, throwing those imaginary cards into the zone of the crack.

When you are consistent with both elements, put them together. If you do it with good timing, the elements will coincide and you will cut a thrown card with a single crack of your whip.

It is the timing which counts. You will need to begin the circus crack before you throw the card. It's not that you are knocking the card out of the air with the whip – you are throwing the card *into* the whip's crack.

Stick a full deck of cards into your belt on your throwing hand's side. You can pull cards one at a time from the box until you have run through the whole deck. This is a lot easier than trying to hold the deck in your hand and tossing the cards individually. Get a predictable rhythm going.

In an ideal, perfect universe, you could hypothetically make your aim and timing consistent enough to perform this trick blindfolded.

Candle Snuffing

Set the candle chest high on a stable surface. If you need to, tape the stand down. If you touch the candlestick, you will knock it over and send a waterfall of wax cascading to the floor.

Make sure the wick is high enough to light. If you have used the candle for this before, you may have knocked the wick down to a nub.

With each individual crack, you create three chances to snuff the candle.

If you snuff a candle with an Overhand Flick, aim slightly above the flame. At the end of the throw, hold your hand still so the crack occurs precisely above the flame. Here's the cheat: if the shock wave created by the cracker pushing the air is not sufficient to put the flame out by itself, momentum will cause the cracker to drop down and blow a breeze over the wick, putting the flame out. At worst, the cracker will drop down to physically stroke the top of the wick, extinguishing the flame. Not pretty, but effective. Try to do better next time.

If you are using a Circus Crack, aim slightly below the flame. Once again, if the push of air from the shock wave of the crack is not sufficient to extinguish the flame, the breeze blown by the moving cracker will do the job. At worst, the tips of the cracker will knock the flame out.

The size of the candle has nothing to do with the trick. This will work with huge cathedral candles or tiny birthday candles.

If you use an assistant to hold a candle, make sure she holds the candle out to her side and not in front of herself. You do not want to splash candle wax into her eyes or onto her costume.

Slicing a Banana

Have your holder grip the banana tightly or it will go flying when it is hit. The banana needs to be absolutely still or it will merely absorb the blow and not slice. The grip should be a tight clasp, all the way around the banana near the end or the hand will act as a shock absorber, preventing the cut. If the banana is dangled by the fingertips, it will simply be knocked to the floor.

A shorter whip will put you closer to the target.

Use a firm banana. A soft banana will split or explode. You want a clean, knife-like slice. If the fruit is soft, a blow will puree the contents, which will absorb the crack. If you chill a fresh banana, it cuts cleaner.

Aim for the end of the banana. Give your assistant a margin for safety. Have her angle the banana slightly so it is parallel to the floor, giving you more length to shoot for with a horizontal stroke.

Make sure your stroke is horizontal and does not cross the plane of the assistant's body at any point – it doesn't look good to hit her in the knees after you slice the banana.

Use a thinner (sharper) cracker about 6 inches long.

Hit the banana with an Overhand Flick and add a squeezed-handle grace note to supercharge the crack.

Try to lay the cracker in so the banana is hit across the middle of the cracker and does not touch the fall. If the banana is hit by the fall or any other part of the whip, it will explode as surely as if Gallagher had hit it with a sledge hammer. If I'm having a good night, I can take slices off the banana an inch or two at a time.

This trick is best for an adult audience, because of the phallic overtones. If your assistant holds the banana at groin level, out of the corners of your eyes you will see men jerk their knees together when you slice the banana.

Build the tension. Do wraps on the banana first, slow and sensual. This way, when you slice the banana, it is a greater shock.

Make sure the stage manager knows to clean the stage of banana afterward, especially if you are being followed by dancers. The remains of the banana could be dangerous to the performer who follows you. The joke of someone slipping on a banana peel is not funny when it is another performer being messed up because you did not take responsibility for the consequences of your own act. Be considerate. If you're in a show, you're part of a team.

Newspaper Cutting

A good newspaper cut begins before you start throwing the whip at the newspaper.

You have to pick your newspaper carefully. A typical newspaper has some pages which are printed on thinner paper than others. Color pages (grocery ads) tend to be thicker sheets, which are harder to cut. The

Dante and Kim perform in San Diego

ideal newspaper is a wafer thin overseas edition. There is no need to pre-crease the newspaper page.

Your assistant should hold the page by the top two corners firmly, pulling slightly to make the edge of the paper tight. If the top edge is not tight, the whip will strike the soft paper and merely crumple the paper. You want it to slice. Usually, a crack will slice the page, but if there is a little outward pressure, the assistant can complete a partial slice by manually separating the sheet the rest of the way.

Gery Deer plays with this blindfolded. His assistant Scout tears the newspaper even though he deliberately and obviously misses it by a mile. Gery can actually cut a newspaper down to postage stamp size if he wants to, but sometimes it's just more entertaining this way.

The fine whip cracker Chris (The Whip Guy) Camp told me he'd heard of a bullwhip artist who ran his newspapers through a sewing machine so the paper would cut along the perforated line. The trouble with this is that it makes it easier for the paper to split at the slightest pressure, making folks think the whole stunt is a sham. The best way to do it is the right way, the pure way – actually cut the paper.

From Dante's notebook: It seems to me that every time someone tries to introduce a "cheat" into a trick, all they do is introduce one more way for the trick to screw up.

Let's get back to the actual stunt:

The assistant's arms should be fully extended, holding the newspaper as far away from her body as possible.

As each crack slices the paper down the middle, the assistant should crumple one half of the used sheet in one hand and hold the remaining paper at *precisely* the same point in space so the whip cracker does not need to take aim afresh every time. Each new smaller rectangle of newspaper should be held at the upper two corners in order to create a firm, tight edge for the whip to slice through. *The long edge of the rectangle should always be held horizontally, to present a larger target for the whip.* The possibility of a partial cut diminishes with each successive cut, since the pieces are getting smaller and the whip's cracker has more chance to travel through the whole scrap.

When the page has been sliced three or four times or when the assistant gets nervous, she can now turn her body slightly so that she is holding the piece of newspaper like a playing card (review that trick, above). The secret here is that she holds the scrap of paper at precisely the same point in space that she held the full newspaper. The whip cracker does not need to take aim from scratch.

A circus crack works best for this one. Bring the whip up on a specific line and bring it back down on precisely the same line. Use the rising stroke to line the whip up so you don't have to adjust your aim every time.

The rhythm of this trick is important. One crack for distance, one crack to cut, one crack for distance, one crack to cut, one crack for distance, one crack to cut. Bang-Bang-Bang-Bang for two cuts. The "distance crack" is the pause your assistant needs to reposition the paper for the next slicing crack.

You avoid hitting her on the upswing by not extending your arm fully, and by rocking slightly back on the distance crack, and then leaning forward slightly for the cutting stroke.

It's an individual matter of how small to make the last piece. Some folks like to get it down to a business card size, but some folks like to take this even smaller. You can keep going until the last cut disappears from the Assistant's fingers because she lets go, in which case she should smile beamingly and show her empty hand to the audience. This also proves she still has all her fingers!

Slicing a newspaper off a person's back without nicking them is an edgy trick which freaks people out because of its S&M overtones – it's a politically incorrect showstopper, and it should probably be the last trick in your performance because it's a tough one to top.

Prepare a sheet of newspaper before the performance. Put strips of duct tape along the outside edges of the short sides of the newspaper. Overlap the paper so that half of the tape's sticky side extends past the paper.

When the moment comes for this trick, have your Assistant remove her top or coat or otherwise bare her back. Take the prepared newspaper page and attach one strip of tape across her back so the newspaper hangs loosely down her back.

Have the Assistant stretch her hands out to her sides, slightly forward. She should now push her tummy forward and her butt backward. Attach the bottom of the newspaper to her buttocks.

Look like you are adjusting the newspaper, while you are really curling the long sides of the newspaper slightly away from her body. This is to better catch the cracker when you throw the whip in her direction.

If you look at your Assistant sideways, you will see that because of her posture, the newspaper hangs straight down but her body is curled in a serpentine fashion. She should look like a capital letter D – there should be a sizable hollow space between her back and the newspaper. This is your margin of error.

Use side-arm shots sent out absolutely parallel to the ground. Crack the whip outside the newspaper, following through on a flat trajectory until you touch the paper. Be prepared to move to the left or right to get a right angle. She should not move at all.

You should just brush the outside edge of the newspaper and nick it without touching her back. Once an initial cut is started, you can continue to tear the paper by just touching the end of the rip in the paper. After three or four of these, the paper will fall into two pieces. If it doesn't, proclaim the end of the trick by walking over to her and carefully removing the newspaper. Hold the shredded sheet up to the audience with one hand as you perform a Vanna White hand movement to indicate your Assistant's back is unscathed. At this point she should turn, smiling to the audience. You may both bow.

The hardest part of this stunt is to safely get that initial cut started.

It is vital in this trick that you know your distance. Practice with the same whip you will be using in performance. Practice with the same length of cracker. Make sure your Assistant understands how important it is to not move forward or back, even slightly. She should maintain the same posture throughout the performance of this number. If she shrugs or adjusts her position, the tape may come loose and allow the newspaper to lie flat against her back. There will be no margin for safety. If the trick is performed correctly, the newspaper catches all the strokes. It is not necessary for your Assistant to be a masochist – just a brave person. But you'd better be spot on!

Wraps and Grabs

To snatch and grab something from someone's hand like a knife or sword, do a gentle wrap. Lock the fall with a flip and pull. You'll get to the point that you can make the crack occur simultaneously.

Watch your face! The object you grab will come sailing back at you, so be prepared to catch it. In my act, I've used a realistic looking plastic knife, and it would not do to skewer myself before the end of a performance! If you strike with too much momentum in the whip, you will slap the object hard and probably just knock it out of your assistant's hand. There's no art to this.

Go gently but firmly. You can still get the loud crack, but it is more impressive when executed with grace. It's more accurate, as well.

From Dante's notebook: I love to do this with scarves, usually made of chiffon. Silk slips too easily and is so heavy the whip does not have a chance to grab it.

If the scarf wraps around the fall and follows it, I can do a circus crack forward and make the scarf fly off the whip back into the air. When I play, I like to see how long I can keep a scarf airborne.

With Assistant: A Bullwhip Tango

This choreographed dance consists of wraps of hand, leg, waist, over shoulder. The wraps are circus cracks, rising cracks, side shots and backhand shots. The Assistant should be ready to spin to release the whip. Wraps can be done on an arm, wrist, and ultimately on an individual finger. Wraps include double self wraps (a good closing). If performed with two whips simultaneously, bear in mind that waist wraps from both sides will be awkward to remove.

Double-handed wraps from the same side (a side shot and a back hand, coming from the same side) can be performed to wrap the knees and waist at the same time. The advantage to wrapping on the same side is the assistant can facilitate the release by spinning in a single direction.

The tango itself is the basis of this routine and the whip cracker and Assistant should be prepared to "dance" with each other in this one, with the whips.

Dante and Tina perform bullwhip dance

With Assistant: Styrofoam Strip Cutting

Styrofoam strips are better than spaghetti, even if you have to clean up afterward (or have a stage hand handy with a fast broom).

Get styrofoam plates from a grocery store meat department. From a single large plate, you can cut about a dozen strips with a razor or sharp knife. Because they are brittle, I transport them in a round wine box.

Styrofoam plates come in all colors, but opt for the lighter colors (yellow, orange, white). Strips made from these colors are easier for audiences to see.

When I carry strips in my own inside vest pocket, I put them in a stiff cardboard sleeve to prevent their breaking while I'm moving. If you use blacklight whips, you can decorate the strips with fluorescent paint or UV markers to make them glow under the blacklights like the nylon whips.

Tip: you can very slightly score a strip to break at a certain point, usually the middle. Barely break the surface tension on one wide side and one thin side. If you don't, a cutting crack that is not super-precise will make the strip break where it is being held. If this happens, a showman whip cracker can smile is if he intended to cut the strip that close to his assistant's fingers. But personally, I like a clean cut. The advantage of a scored strip is that after you have cut it, if you are really good, you can cut it again. It will likely "cut" right at your assistant's fingers.

Reminder: In *any* trick with another person, make sure you are good enough to do it alone before you even try it with someone else. Master this trick

Tina gets her strips ready

without an assistant, first. The whole chemistry changes when you start throwing your whip in the direction of a human being. Get used to that fact before you try anything fancy. Have them wear a leather jacket. Remember to use goggles or a face mask. Have them wear leather gloves. Push the envelope only in practice – an audience has not paid to see you screw up so always perform slightly below your level of capability.

Here are some variations on a simple styrofoam strip cut:

Straight Cut: Assistant holds styrofoam strip out in hand. You cut it. Ta daa!

Cut from Mouth: Assistant holds styrofoam strip in mouth. Trick here is to make sure the styrofoam strip is parallel to the floor, thin edge upward. Make sure the strip is long enough to give a margin of safety.

Speed Cuts: Assistant holds styrofoam strips between fingers in both hands, and angles them to be cut one at a time with consecutive cracks.

Three Strips at Once: Assistant holds styrofoam strips parallel in mouth and in both hands, all three above each other so that one circus crack cuts all three.

Two-handed Strip Cutting: Using behind-the-back hand switch, whip handler cracks consecutive styrofoam strips held alternately in left and right hands of Assistant. Go through 6 or 8 strips.

Contortionist Cuts: Assistant vamps with styrofoam strip, hitting sexy, tense poses which allow the whip cracker to target the styrofoam strips to be cut with single cracks. Adapt this to the age of your audience.

With Assistant: Cracking a Coin Off a Tongue

Warning: This is very dangerous! Do not try this at all!

The only reason I even mention it is that it *can* be done, but *not* by beginners, amateurs or the merely foolhardy. Leave it for the professionals. You can slash a cheek or put an eye out. Simply: don't do it!

Reread that first paragraph. Now continue.

Coin or poker chip is placed on Assistant's tongue. She angles her head back and sticks her tongue out sufficiently to allow the whip to clear her nose. Using the "Point and Squeeze" technique, the whip is cracked first loudly, then gingerly as a delicate wrap so that only the soft momentum of the fall actually knocks the coin off the tongue.

From Dante's notebook: This is on video done by the great Australian whip artist John Brady and his lovely wife Vi. A classic!

With Assistant: Flying Streamer Cut

To prepare, tie a weight to the end of a length of string; then attach a long crepe streamer to the weight.

The Assistant swings the streamer in a big circle using her whole arm slowly enough to keep the string tight. As she swings, the whip handler cracks and cuts pieces off the end of the streamer, again and again.

One hypothetical sequence calls for four distinct cuts:

The first is with the Assistant making a vertical circle in front of herself.

In the second cut, she spins the streamer vertically beside her body so it comes up toward the whip cracker who cuts it with a side shot.

Still spinning the streamer, she now swings it on the horizontal plane above her head. The whip cracker cuts it with an Overhand Flick or circus crack. The Assistant should make sure she extends her arm to keep the whip a safe distance from her.

In the final cut, she continues spinning the streamer vertically in front of herself. The whip cracker cuts it again and again until there is nothing left to cut.

At this point, the Assistant should let the string ground out and raise her arms to the audience, signifying the end of the trick.

From Dante's notebook: I like to use poi to practice this and to perform. I attach crepe streamers from a party store with duck tape. I stretch the duration of this otherwise brief trick out if I target the tail end and get numerous cuts out of a single routine.

To get the timing down, practice. You will see that you should start your crack when the poi bag is behind or on the opposite side of your assistant.

This is a relatively safe stunt. Remember that the whip will follow through after it cuts, so make sure your partner is in the "safe zone" for your entire stroke, even to the follow-through. Think ahead!

Ch. 9 – Performing

Character – Choreography – Rehearsing – Using Blacklights –Costume Tips – Finding a Good Assistant – Venues – Handling Tangled Lashes - Dancing on the Edge

"Do the thing, and you have the power!" Emerson

I received a call recently, asking me if I would appear at a charity benefit function. I instantly agreed (this isn't all about money, you know), and I asked about the parameters for our appearance.

What's the date and time? How long do we perform? What's the space like? Who's the audience? What's the lighting? Is there a sound system? Do I do patter or do I work mute? Do we supply our own music or is there a DJ?

If this had been a paying gig, we would have talked about money, at this point or earlier. If money had been a factor, we would have discussed a contract or a letter of commitment.

Let's say someone asks you to crack your whip at their event, fundraiser or party. How do you do this in such a way that it is entertaining, safe and enjoyable for everyone, including you?

The answer is to be a professional about it. This means your work begins long before you set one foot onto a stage.

Character

Just doing tricks is not performing. I have seen many technically excellent but lifeless and limp whip performances. Expensive costumes by themselves are not enough to compensate for a listless presentation.

Get yourself a character to be when you perform. It can be almost anything. There are vampire whip crackers, cosmic cowgirls, clowns, Indians, gunslingers, Celts in kilts.

Ideally, the character will be an extension of yourself –you'll never have to worry about breaking character.

Most experts agree that this is the most important question of all: "What is my character?" As Andrew Conway says, "An act begins with the character, not the tricks."

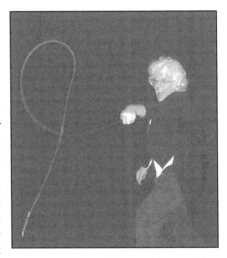

A Dante 'Wild Tuxedo' show in LA

He's right.

Ask yourself, "Who am I performing?" Even Nietzsche noted that where most people saw a so-called "great man," he consistently saw an ordinary man acting out his own ideal image of himself. Do it consciously and claim the power to be great!

Your character will give you a sense of identity in front of an audience and give them someone they can relate to on some level at first sight. Tailor your tricks to express this character.

Joyce Rice was a national champion baton twirler when she was a youngster so it was natural for her to prefer to use shorter whips and to incorporate flips, twirls and twists into her routines. Her routines are bright, bouncy, giddy and gleeful affairs.

I'm lucky – when I perform, I perform My Self, exaggerated. I am arrogant, pompous, "eat up with myself," as Southerners would say. I act like I think I am the bee's knees. This way, when my Assistant pops my self-delusional balloon and brings me back down to earth, it's a satisfying experience for everyone.   We all like to see someone get his

116

comeuppance. The key here is to be abashed and amused, to laugh at myself. This takes the cruelty out of it and makes it a morality play. It humanizes my Assistant, too, as she twits me like Tinkerbelle on behalf of the audience. And it allows folks to look past the monstrous cardboard-front ego to see the very real skill and professionalism from both of us. By the end of the show, they see quite clearly that we are a Team. And that we had Fun getting there.

Choreography

Others do it differently (and so will you), but here's how I do it.

First, I've got the gig. Now, I ask myself some important questions: How long do I have? What is the space like? What is the audience like? Is it a mute show or will I be doing patter (talking) as I perform? Who handles the lights? Do I supply music or do they?

I know what tricks I can perform safely, and I have a repertoire of stories with which to regale the audience. I get out my stopwatch, a pad and pencil.

Let's say they want 10 minutes with no patter, a straight circus performance or nightclub variety act.

First, I break the 10 minutes into segments. For example, for a 10-minute show, I'll open with a 90-second solo whip cracking routine, starting simply with a single whip, and then moving into two-handed cracking. Even though I have already warmed up, I'll use the easy stuff to help me get into the groove. While I am doing this, my Assistant sets up on the other side of the stage, lighting candles, preparing styrofoam strips, whatever. She is quick, efficient and inconspicuous with her business, because otherwise she will draw attention away from you. It's a trade-off, so she should minimize her non-performing activity.

I always give the audience a chance to express its appreciation. I give permission to applaud with a pause, a smile or a pose. A fast volley routine which stops with a couple of loud cracks in the middle and then continues will get as much applause in the middle of a performance as it does at the end. (Thank you, Andrew, for the suggestion!) Even if it's not perfect, there's always enough worth applauding. It's entertainment, not the Olympics.

As Franz Liszt said, "Don't let your desire to hit the right notes get in the way of the music."

If you screw up, don't pretend it didn't happen. The audience saw it, so play with it. Try again, with a shrug and big smile, or a joke. This keeps the audience from being embarrassed for you, and it shows that you are still in control of the show. This is vital for the audience to continue to have confidence in you.

If my aim is slightly off and I have crack several times without touching the target held by my assistant, I may pause, scratch my head, look up and squint as though I am trying to see where the light is. I then walk forward to take my assistant's shoulders in my hands and to move her *two inches* to her left. I walk back to my spot and sight down my whip, pretending it was her fault all the time for not standing in the exactly right place. This fits my persona, as well. By this time, the spell is broken, and the cut usually follows precisely and quickly. And the audience thinks it is part of the act.

Three is good number of times to try to get a trick. The second try raises the tension level, which is relieved when it is successfully executed on the third try. If you can't do it on the third try, substitute a simpler trick and move on.

Sometimes, the knots on your whips will tangle. This is why it's a good idea to have several whips with you – matched pairs are perfect. Go with the flow, keep it moving. You're on a schedule, and you can't lose the audience for a moment!

Keeping all this in mind, I've still got 7 or so minutes left to choreograph.

Cutting a newspaper, popping balloons, slicing a playing card and capping it all with a candle snuffing routine will take 3 minutes. This leaves me 4 minutes to fill.

At this point I can take one minute to indulge in a sensual tango-style dance utilizing wraps and allowing the audience to enjoy the beauty of my Assistant, which is also appropriate to my "character." Even at the end of this section, we always remember to bow – both of us. This lets the audience know this section is over and the next is about to begin.

I now have 3 minutes to go. I can take 1 minute to display some self-cutting tricks. This leaves me 2 minutes. I can now do the cutting-newspaper-off-back trick. I give myself 30 seconds to build the tension, place the newspaper. I give myself 45 seconds to accomplish the cutting. This leaves me 45 seconds for problems, or to sell the trick even more. It's my call when I see what the moment holds.

There's my hypothetical 10-minute routine.

Not every show is put together the same way. You need to grab the audience first, and your second-best trick is a good way to start. But your best trick should be your closer, leaving the audience wanting more. Oddly, your best trick may not be the the the most difficult one – judge by audience satisfaction, the "Wow!" factor.

Since it's a mute show, I need music. I obtained royalty-free music from a commercial house, but you can also find it over the internet or from a record shop.

These CDs have music for magicians or commercials and so on, broken down into 10- and 20-second segments

A band on stage? No problem!

and longer. They offer different flavors of music for different purposes. I pick the music I need for each segment in 2- and 3-minute increments. I rehearse to the music, so I will be able to keep track of where I am in my performance by knowing the music. I choose dramatic, driving melodies. The nice thing about this type of "canned music" is that the sections dovetail into each other, allowing me to create the music which best fits my routine.

Equally important is to make sure everything works together. If my show is for a Western venue, I don't wear my tails and vampire vest and play Goth music. Your costume should reflect your character.

If it's a 5-minute routine with patter, I don't try to cram everything I know into the 5 minutes. I may use a specifically choreographed routine with a gimmick like a blindfold. Something like this will allow me to use a 3-minute routine to fill 5 minutes. In this case, by the way, the tricks are the same, basically, but the Assistant uses a "clicker" toy to tell me where to crack. I do a "distance crack," and she knows that is where the next crack is coming. She positions the object to be cut like a styrofoam strip precisely on that same line. Especially in risky routines, I try to make the safety factor as large as possible. Any stunt with a bullwhip is dangerous enough by itself. Stack the odds in your favor.

I enjoy the luxury of working with Tina who also cracks whips. As a professional belly dancer, she knows how to move so that when she cracks a whip, it becomes a sensual, mesmerizing moment that I could not hope to achieve. It expands our possibilities and she's an equal partner in the act. She also performs solo, but it's always a better show when we work together.

_____

Rehearsing

Don't leave anything to chance. Rehearse the individual elements of a performance, and then rehearse how they go together. Don't assume a thing. With my Assistant, I even practice walking onstage. We practice bows. We practice in costumes. When we do our final dress rehearsal, we practice everything from the dressing room to the stage and back.

It is important to practice to the music. I like to get it down so completely that the music will tell me which trick comes next and how long I have to go before I need to begin the next stunt.

I have used silent signals with some of my Assistants. In my shows, I don't want to shout to my Assistant or wave my hand like a traffic cop so our signals are basic and easy to remember. Here are two of my signals: if I touch my nose, it means she is standing too close and she needs to move further away from me. She should respond naturally, not giving an indication that she has received a message from me. If I reach across my body to scratch my arm, it means I need her to move closer to me. She can make her final adjustment in relation to the sound of the whip cracking off to her side in my "distance crack" set-up.

It helps to make the signals intuitive, natural. The "move back" signal of touching/holding my nose is the same as saying "I don't like the smell of this." Holding my arm across my body almost like I'm hugging myself means "I need a hug," which means I want her to move closer to me. Please don't read more into this than I intend – a professional does not mix Church and State. Your Assistant is your working partner, not your love bunny.

_____

Using Blacklights

Find a good whip maker who crafts whips out of nylon. Ask to see samples of the colored nylon they use to braid their whips. Run these samples under a blacklight to see which ones glow. Get your whips made of this material.

I got a pair of 5-foot Florida cow whips from whip maker Rhett Kelly of Georgia. Working with them was laborious, because of the clunky traditional handles. I noticed the thongs also seemed to be heavier than they had to be, but this made the whips strike out more quickly, ensuring greater accuracy for this style of whip.

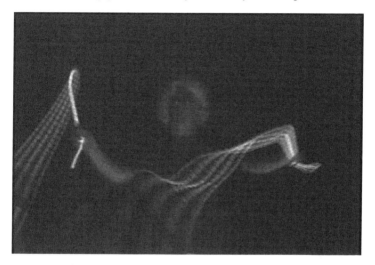

Blacklight whips leave "trails" in the air. Very dramatic!

I removed the handles and put the thongs onto an ordinary pair of stock whip handles, and the whips worked beautifully. I could now do cutting tricks and two-handed whip cracking routines I desired. I have heard that Rhett now makes his whips lighter so they move more like Australian 'roo whips, and he now makes nylon bullwhips, as well.

I use whips made by Dave King of Coyote Whips, and I love them. I have found other whip makers who seem to have the knack, and that club is growing. It includes Jesse Gallagher of Loko Whips and Noreast Whips based in New England.

The bright yellow nylon of the thongs glows electrically under a blacklight. Because of the number of times per second the blacklight cycles, the whips leave "trails," a stroboscopic memory of the whip's movement. This can be distracting when you work with them, so make sure you can do it with your eyes closed. You will rely on feeling more than sight with these whips under blacklight.

I use blacklight makeup in my hair and wear phosphorescent clothing. If I didn't, the whips would appear to float in space. If my

Assistant is working me, we use styrofoam strips which have been sprayed with glow-in-the-dark paint. The same spray paint is used on playing cards and newspaper for other tricks.

Blacklights only work if the audience sees the object bathed in the UV light. If your shadow covers the blacklight, the object will stop glowing. It helps to have blacklights coming at you from at least two directions. The rest of the room should be as dark as possible to maximize the blacklight effect. Some paints glow under blacklights. Use these for your props. Florescent paint and objects actually increase their glow as they are exposed to blacklight.

Try to keep your nylon whips off the floor. These whips get dirty easily. If they get dirty, their reactivity to blacklight diminishes. Store them in plastic bags or pillow cases. When traveling, wrap the thongs in plastic bags to prevent leather conditioner from other whips from darkening the nylon strands.

I have tossed nylon whips into a washing machine after placing them in a pillow case. I was worried about this weakening the braiding and allowing the shot loading to break loose, but this has not happened yet. I've also used spray cleaners on them with positive results. A good whip maker's work is sturdy, thank goodness!

Costume tips

Dress for the venue. Cowboy clothes for rodeo, vampire formal for Goth club shows, whatever is appropriate.

Practice in your costumes. Some spinning moves may not work with tuxedo tails, for example. High heels or clunky boots on your Assistant

Will the audience watch me or my Assistant?

may look sexy but not if it puts her off balance. One wrap at an off-balance moment and she could tumble to the floor.

Keep your costumes clean and pressed. You're a professional, so dress accordingly. Your hosts don't want someone in jeans and sneakers. They want to feel like they're getting their money's worth.

Avoid costumes that restrict movement. With a whip, you're going to need to move freely. If gloves are worn, make them as skin-tight as possible so dexterity is not compromised.

Avoid danglies and banglies and things that hang off a costume. Your whip will catch on these, for sure, and *always* at the worst moment.

When you travel, take several choices of costumes. It doesn't help to show up to do a show with only an all-black outfit just to see the curtain behind you is all-black as well. You will be a floating head as your costume disappears into the background.

Look at many other performers from all genres. *This LA TV show called for a Wild West theme.* Good ideas can be found with ice skaters, circus performers, magicians, movies and books.

Finding a Good Assistant

What does it take to be a Bullwhip Assistant?

More than you might think, because a good bullwhip act is made up of a good whip cracker and a good "Holder" or Assistant, or "Target Girl." It really does take two to tango!

There are definitely good solo acts (Vince Bruce and Joyce Rice leap to mind), and performers like Chris Camp who use volunteers from the audience very effectively.

If you use an assistant, understand she does not just hold and pose. She (or he) is as important to the success of a performance as the supposed star is. In reality, you are both stars.

Here's what I look for:

Intelligence: A good holder knows as much about the bullwhip as the performer does. Assuming the Assistant is female, we can say that she knows how to care for their whips. She knows what to look for in a whip. She probably knows how to crack whips, herself (or she wants to learn).

Knowing as much as the whip cracker does, she can anticipate what is going to happen in a performance and can adapt her movements to meet the needs of the venue (i.e. Where are the lights? Can the audience see everything? Is the area safe for performing sometimes risky maneuvers?)

The luxury of a nice big stage!

A good holder understands acceptable risks and will approach dangerous stunts with caution. A good holder will not take chances or risks in a bullwhip show. A good holder can, however, stack the odds in her favor, and the closer she can make those odds 100-percent, the better the act. Being brave does not mean being stupid, even though courage is a prerequisite!

Look for a Dancer, a Performer: The great whip cracker Brian Chic told me he found good assistants and partners at dance studios, and I can understand this.

She knows how to move gracefully (and in an adult show, erotically). She has impeccable timing since she is moving with the whips. She also has good comedic timing in order to play with the audience. And she knows how to dance with her partner, the whip cracker. A top-notch bullwhip performance is a duet because she must be an *active* partner. She can't just stand there like a mannequin or the audience will fall asleep, no matter how good the whip cracker is!

The assistant "sells" the trick to the audience. She helps to set up the routine and then helps the audience appreciate what has happened. She is the divine or impish intermediary between the whip cracker and the Audience. She is their guide, the one who makes the human contact with the Audience. Few audience members can relate to the whip cracker, especially if he is very good. But they can empathize with the lovely young lady! They sympathize with her, they fear for her, they have concern for her - she is their heroine! They rejoice when she escapes unharmed! They delight in her courage much more than they appreciate the whip cracker's skills!

124

Beauty is in the Eye of the Beholders: A live performer is only as good as she can be on her worst day. This means she watches her diet, she does not overindulge in intoxicants or stimulants, she exercises and she gets enough sound sleep. Of course, this holds true for the whip cracker, as well!

In performance and rehearsal, one should be completely in the moment and alert. Any intoxicant or stimulant will throw this off.

As politically incorrect as it appears, a sexy assistant can provide "eye candy" for a performance and this can work to a performer's advantage.

A magician's assistant traditionally dresses in skimpy or erotic clothing to distract the audience. With a bullwhip artist, beauty and vulnerability make stunts seem more dangerous, so the "payoff" is more satisfying when she escapes harm. She distracts the audience from any mundane stage business which accompanies a particular performance. She emphasizes the erotic aura which surrounds daredevils. Fear is arousing, and people want to be thrilled, entertained.

An Indy-like body twist adds drama

Look for a Professional Attitude: To do this with integrity and passion, you've got to want to do it more than just about anything else in your life. Bullwhip performing is a craft and a skill, but it is Show Business as much as it is a demonstration of technical accuracy. The first job of the Assistant and the whip cracker is to entertain. The whip is merely the vehicle by which this is accomplished. This is supported by using costumes, lights, music, performance skills, intelligent choreography, well written scripts and well executed performances which are the result of rehearsals, rehearsals and more rehearsals.

A good Assistant is both Realistic AND Idealistic. A bullwhip act is a romantic adventure with intangible rewards which are greatly satisfying. You may not get rich doing this but you may be able to make a living. Many performers use whips as an adjunct to other skills, such as trick roping, juggling, knife throwing, magic, trick riding or stunt work. In my own life, I have found that private lessons, group demos and sales of bullwhip-related products account for a sizable portion of my performing income.

Professional athletes put their uniforms on and show up for the game even if they don't feel like being in the stadium that day. They are on time, they are courteous, they deliver what they are paid to provide. When they do their jobs right, people want to come and see them again and again. They are constantly trying to raise their levels of excellence. The good ones don't believe their own propaganda. They know they are only as good as their last game so the top pros are the ones who are out there practicing, every day, not only because they love the game but also because they know they have to work to become the best and to stay the best.

Balancing Reality and Artistry: Do not have any illusions: this is a hard life. You're never as good as you want to be. You will be criticized for things not in your control. If something can screw up in a performance, it probably will and in ways you can not anticipate. You will be critical of yourself as you try to perfect your technique and skill. You can't let yourself get away with a single thing because the audience won't. You have to have the heart of a warrior, a crusader, a samurai. You have to be committed to your vision and your partner. The Act must come first. You must be willing to sacrifice. Yes, on a weekend you might want to get away to the beach, but a show set for Saturday night cannot be rescheduled.

An Assistant brings her passion and her creativity to the act. She watches other performers in other disciplines and applies what she sees to her own act. There may be days when one thinks that no activity is worth such effort and inconvenience, but then there comes that moment when a facial expression of someone watching makes you realize that the whole experience is surpassing your wildest dreams.

A good bullwhip act is made up of a good whip cracker and a good assistant. No bullwhip artist or magician can do it alone. The assistant is as important to the success of the performance as the whip cracker.

Venues

Most bullwhip artists perform at rodeos and Wild West shows for family-oriented audiences but there are other venues, including circuses, county fairs, art fairs, cruise ships, corporate events, theme parks, private parties and adult-oriented Goth/Fetish/BDSM events. There are also burlesque shows (the modern equivalent of vaudeville) and nightclub gigs.

I've performed at charity shows and fetish fashion shows with only slight changes necessary to make the presentations suit the differing audiences.

In this case, it really is a case of "It's not what you do, it's the way that you do it."

Dante & Kim at a WWAC convention

Whip Tips: Handling Tangled Lashes

A young friend in Ohio wrote to me about a show he did.

Sure enough, the nightmare of all professional bullwhip artists happened to him: he knotted his cracker and fall.

Fortunately, he had the presence of mind to relate a funny story while he did his fast repair and he resumed his performance without losing the audience.

There are things you can do to minimize pitfalls:

1. Do not condition your whip less than 24 hours before a show. The conditioner makes the fall "tacky" and it wants to grab your cracker

2. Do have a backup whip you can grab quickly. Ideally, it is identical to the first whip, a matched pair.

3. Shorten your cracker. Longer crackers are more likely to tangle. Practice cutting with shorter crackers because the depth will be slightly different.

4. Learn to 'set' your whip or 'ground' it a lot during a show. This makes your shots straighter and less loopy. Do it fluidly to keep the whip moving with style.

5. Get a good couple of good comedy schticks to use if a whip tangles. The main rule for a performer is that it's almost okay if you crash and burn just as long as you are entertaining about it. The truth is that the venue isn't paying you to be a superb whip handler; they are paying you to entertain the audience. And just as you'll never find a juggler who has never dropped a ball, you will probably never meet a pro bullwhip handler who doesn't have some story about a tangled whip, a chandelier or the like.

Your Invitation to the Dance

So if you enjoy traveling, if you are exhibitionistic, if you like people and like to meet people, if you'd like to do something few people have done, if you'd like to create memories for a lifetime, if this sort of life sounds exciting to you, this your invitation to The Dance!

Let's Get Cracking!

Brenda exults in the joy of whip cracking!

Ch. 10 – DANCING ON THE EDGE

(Professional Bullwhip Assistant Tina talks about being on the other side of the whip.)
You Do What? – Oh, I Could Never Do That – Relationships & Communication – It's Easier Than You Think

You Do What...?

I am asked many times, "Why do you do what you do?"

I know accounting is safer than standing in front of a weapon that breaks the sound barrier, or letting someone throw knives in my direction, or squeezing into a small space for the sake of entertainment.

The short answer is that I do these things because I can - and because for me they are fun.

But it's not just me. I believe there is a Special Something in each of us that allows us to do things other people consider insane, risky or foolish. I also believe that there is a Special Something in all of us that finds insane, risky and foolish things entertaining.

Risk, however, is a relative thing; one person's risk is another person's adventure.

On any given day, it's usually safer to stand at a target board than to cross a street in midtown Manhattan. When I perform a 'dangerous' act, conditions are hyper-focused on safety, and rightfully so. Yes, you go in with the awareness that something could happen. The bullwhip has tagged me and the knife has grazed me. Recently I lost my balance and fell four feet off an illusion during a magic performance. These incidents took me less by surprise than when I was rear-ended on the freeway.

129

Oh, I Could Never Do That...

As a whip and knife thrower's assistant, I usually encounter three reactions: 'Wow, that's cool!'; 'Wow, that's crazy!'; and 'Wow, I wanna try that!'

Three types of people say they "wanna try that": Those who say they want to and don't; Those who say they want to and try it once; And those who say they want to see if it's something they'd like to pursue further.

My assisting in the whip act arose from curiosity and sense of adventure, along with a love for being on stage. Dante and I met because he needed an assistant for a performance and I found his graceful handling of the whip very captivating (and his accuracy reassuring!) The knives came next, and then stage magic, each new experience building on the one that went before.

What does it take to be a good assistant? Sure, bravery, confidence and trust top the list. But just as important are effective communication skills, strong stage presence, an open mind and a willingness to be vulnerable in an empowered way. (In illusion work, flexibility also is a strong plus.)

Whips, knife throwing and magic can be done without an assistant, but my presence adds dynamism by increasing the perceived risk level, therefore the excitement. A passive assistant doesn't interplay with audience or the primary "star." An active assistant is more interactive and interpersonal with both the audience and the primary performer.

The assistant is often a partner who creates, collaborates and shares the vision of the act, from choreographing to marketing. The assistant, like the primary performer, constantly represents the act to the public. A great performer doesn't necessarily make a great partner, and vice versa. For some, it's a job. For others, it's a lifestyle.

Relationships & Communication

"Stage Chemistry" is another phrase for the relationship between the primary performer and the assistant. This energy may arise spontaneously or it may need to be developed, but time spent together offstage and in rehearsal will strengthen it. In dangerous acts, this perceived intimacy (whether staged or actual) adds to an audience's sense of risk, vulnerability and power.

In general, an audience assumes there is a power differential when they see someone (typically female) in a vulnerable position, running the risk of being hurt 'by' someone else (typically male). While it may look like dominance and submission, a good assistant is far from 'submissive'. She is there by choice and she is an entity in her own right, whether she does her job without fanfare or establishes a commanding presence from the first moment. In most cases, the assistant will not receive as much credit (or pay!) as the 'star' performer, but their presence is integral to the act. I am lucky to work with performers who acknowledge and appreciate my own work, communicating this to the audience (and to me) on a regular basis.

Communicating and being in tune with each other are the cornerstones of any good performance. This is cultivated onstage and offstage. The acts I work with depend on my awareness of distance, timing and positioning, but it is the responsibility of both performers to know where they are supposed to be and when. This adds to the confidence of the performers. If the show is choreographed to music, music can cue the next trick or tell you to leave one out entirely. Dante can read my arm positions and determine if we have time to finish a leg wrap sequence or whether we should skip it and move right to the neck wrap. Eye contact can indicate the assistant is standing too close. An obvious hand gesture to move back works well, too. A tilt of the head can mean "Give me some more room at the board." In illusion work, face to face communication may be impossible if you are squeezed inside a box, but however it happens, there is always communication.

Communication is especially critical when something isn't going according to plan. How would you react if you were prepared for one rehearsed stunt sequence, but the very real knives flying at you indicated a different stunt? How would you handle it? Making an assumption can have devastating consequences just like any negative energy relating to some off-stage issue, so checking them at the door helps to keep the focus sharp during a show. The safety and success of the act depend on it.

After you make your final bow, take a moment to feel the energy of the audience; appreciate their applause and thank them for the dance. Your onstage partnership extends to them as well. Likewise, take time to thank your partner; giving kudos if it went well and support if it didn't. Once the high abates or the burn wears off from the crash, review the performance to determine what worked and what didn't, and what could have been done to make it better.

It's Easier Than You Think

Doing the act itself is the easy part. During my appearance on Late Night with Conan O'Brien, I had no trouble whipping a flower out of his clenched teeth, but I was a whack of nerves wondering how it would look on the air. During America's Got Talent, my main worry was not that I might forget what I was doing under the bright lights, but that I would trip and fall on my ass as I walked on the stage (negating thirty years of dance training!) in front of a large audience. For those of us who like to show off our exhibitionist side, what happens during a performance occurs relatively naturally. I am in my element, selling the trick and selling myself with a grace and confidence that only comes with discovering that "sweet spot" in my life where everything flows as it should in an unlabored and balanced way. My focus is on engaging the audience, being present for my partner and delivering the best show possible. My hope is to share something new with an audience, or to present an act they might have seen in a way they haven't seen performed before, or to motivate someone to try something they didn't think was possible.

Ten years ago, I did not imagine in my wildest dreams that I'd do what I'm doing. Engaging in experiences that resonate harmonically in my life informs my ability and inspires my confidence to deal with those experiences that don't, and my life is richer for it.

"Empowered Vulnerability" does not stop at the footlights.

Ch. 11 – Teaching and Presenting Workshops

Have safety glasses on hand and make sure people actually wear them.

I suggest you insist that no more than one person at a time crack. Have enough "spotters" to make sure no one walks into harm's way. Some coaches are comfortable handling a half dozen whip crackers at the same time, allowing everyone solo time. When I give a lesson or workshop, I prefer to stay in control of the environment.

Make sure everyone reads the safety rules and signs off on them (you do have safety rules, don't you?). What's the liability situation with insurance, by the way?

Start using the whip immediately to get people used to the sound as you speak about things. The drone of words can get so boring that when you get to the hands-on, the audience is asleep. This won't help.

Target your class. I start every workshop by asking people to raise their hands to show who is a beginner, who is intermediate, and who is advanced. This indicates to me how much I'll need to tailor my presentation so the most people will get the most benefit.

Use tricks and demonstrations to give your words reality. This helps to keep observers interested. If they are falling asleep, they are not learning a thing.

You can demonstrate what is possible with the whip, both positive and negative, by doing some circus tricks to illustrate principles.

More than anything else, know your material inside and out, up and down, forward and back. Review videos and published material (sorry if my name keeps showing up!).

What you will teach is not only how to handle a whip but also the attitude behind its enhanced use. Get straight with yourself and whatever Higher Powers you honor before you step in front of people.

Be Honest. If you don't know the answer, 'fess up. They will respect you more for this than if you give them inaccurate information. No one person knows it all and no amount of arrogance or egoism can obscure this simple truth from those who have eyes to see.

Keep water and snacks on hand. Teaching can be thirsty and intense work. You will work your ass off, but the intangible rewards make the effort worthwhile.

While it is an ideal to do this for free, there are a few of us who actually make our livings performing and teaching. There is nothing wrong with this. I heard once that a patient looked at his surgery bill and asked why his doctor's fee was so high if he was in the operating room for only three hours. The doctor replied, "You're not paying for the three hours. You're paying for my years of college and medical schools, my residencies and internships, my experience and knowledge."

I do a limited number of workshops for costs only, waiving my fees, and I am happy to do this. I do a few freebies during the year to give back to the Universe what has been given to me. I truly wish I could do it this way all the time, but the airlines charge for tickets, the hotels charge for rooms, the restaurants charge for meals, and back home the rent comes due and bills need to be paid. These are the conditions which prevail, as Jimmy Durante said.

The most important teaching tool you have is your own example. Your students subconsciously model their behavior after you, for better or for worse, so make sure you don't do anything you don't want them to do. You are the living picture of whip cracking for them to watch and copy. Your students will do what they see, not what you say.

When you teach, use **Seven Tools to Get Your Message Across:**

1. Be clear. Have your student repeat or show you what you have explained. You'll see quickly enough whether they really have it or not. Be willing to explain Why just as much as How.

2. Be consistent. Repeat yourself again and again, if you have to. Don't worry about sounding like a broken record. You might be hearing yourself say something for the thousandth time, but the person standing beside you may hear it for the first time. Give it a chance to sink in.

3. Think Big. Be obvious, exaggerate your motions. You can show your students how to refine moves into more subtle actions later once they understand principles.

4. Make it easy for the student to make mistakes. This teaches them to solve their own problems so they can move into the right motions. You are teaching them to teach themselves after you leave.

Your goal is to truly teach your student, not for them to merely look good for you or to make you look good. They will be thinking at a thousand miles an hour in the first place, and with this activity too much thinking can get in the way. Humor helps to remove this stress. If you are so good that you never screw up, screw up just a little deliberately. They will learn from seeing you laugh and forgive yourself and then perform the move correctly.

5. Give positive feedback. Give negative feedback one time out of a hundred. Make the other 99 comments positive ones. You can find something to encourage, some slight improvement that shows the person is listening and trying. Make this feedback immediate so its momentum can be taken into the next moment. The folks who are smiling are learning more than the frowners. Use lots of vocal reinforcement, like "That's it! Good!"

6. Keep it interesting. Your student is burning a lot of energy concentrating. Focusing intensely is hard work. This can be draining, and boredom can set in. Repeat problematic moves again and again, breaking it down into its component moves. Then give it a break with something more attainable. They come back to the problem with a fresh mind. This will vary from student to student. Someone with martial arts in their background will have an easier time than someone who is not used to such discipline. Use frequent rests as rewards. Latent learning is a reality. Sometimes it just takes a time for something to sink in.

7. Make the goal Progress, not Perfection. This saves time and will spare you and the student much agony. A beginner will never be perfect. Gradual improvement over time gives the best results. A student is more likely to hang in there long enough to get good if they are not hamstrung by frustration and discouragement, so give your student a history of success by presenting attainable short-term goals in small increments of difficulty. This will build your student's feelings of competence and confidence.

The best thing you can teach your student is how to watch and feel their own whips so they can become self teaching and self correcting.

This is the student who will make you look like you're a good teacher, because if you're doing this, you are a good teacher.

There's no need to apologize for being a good coach or teacher, or for being compensated fairly for teaching. What you offer is valuable. Don't be shy about acknowledging this truth. As they say in Texas, "It ain't brag if it's fact."

As a teacher, your first job is to be a voracious student on behalf of the people you teach. Watch other whip crackers, learn from everyone you can, from dancers to gymnasts to athletes to actors. You are learning not just for yourself but to pass on what you've learned to others. Become the teacher you wish you'd had when you were starting.

Arrogance results in the blind leading the blind. Someone who can do two cracks lords it over those who can perform only one crack. This is a shame because it is so unnecessary.

So, within the parameters of copyright laws, feel free to pass on to others whatever is useful within this book. I have no claim on the truth, but you should make sure that the truth you pass on is your own, honestly earned.

Do this, and I'll shake your hand as a peer. Who knows, you may show me a thing or two I haven't seen before. Do this and we'll both smile, because a pleasure shared is twice the pleasure.

———————————————

Ch. 12 – Practice Routines, Protocols, & Beyond

Practice Routine No. 1 – Practice Routine no. 2 – Safety Protocols – The Perfect Whip Throw – Whips as Exercise – One Dozen Ways to Improve Accuracy – Choreography: Write It Out!

Here are two practice routines and safety protocols for easy reference.

BASIC BULLWHIP PRACTICE ROUTINE NO. 1
BASIC CRACKS

(Single Whip. For right-handed people, "dominant" side is right side; "weak" side is left side. For left-handed people, "dominant" side is left side; "weak" side is right side. Please wear eye protection.)

    A. Setting the Whip
    B. Overhand Flick
    C. Circus Crack
    D. Stockman's Crack

A. Setting the Whip
    Kneel on one knee.
    1) Align whip's belly and roll whip out in front of you with dominant hand. Realign belly and roll whip back behind you. Make sure line is straight and whip does not "slap" floor. Repeat 6 times.
    2) Roll whip with dominant hand on opposite side of body, laying whip out straight in front, then straight behind. Repeat 6 times.
    Switch hands.
    3) Roll whip with weak hand on the weak side of body, laying whip out straight in front, then straight behind. Repeat 6 times.
    4) Roll whip with weak hand on dominant side of body, laying whip out straight in front, then straight behind. Repeat 6 times.

Stand.

5) Align belly and roll whip out in front of you with dominant hand. Roll whip back behind you. Make sure line is straight and whip does not "slap" floor. Repeat 6 times.

6) Align belly and roll whip with dominant hand on the opposite side of body, laying whip out straight in front, then straight behind. Repeat 6 times.

Switch hands.

7) Align belly and roll whip with weak hand on the weak side of body, laying whip out straight in front, then straight behind. Repeat 6 times.

8) Align belly and roll whip with weak hand on dominant side of body, laying whip out straight in front, then straight behind. Repeat 6 times.

B. Overhand Flick

1) Align belly and throw whip straight forward gently with dominant hand. After it cracks, cycle the whip around in a vertical circle on your dominant side until it is behind you, primed to throw forward again. Repeat 6 times.

2) Realign belly and cycle whip on weak side of body with dominant hand (backhand Overhand Flick). After it cracks, cycle the whip around in a vertical circle on your weak side until it is behind you, primed to throw forward again. Repeat 6 times.

Switch hands.

3) Throw whip forward with weak hand on weak side. After it cracks, cycle whip around in a vertical circle on your weak side until it is behind you, primed to throw forward again. Repeat 6 times.

4) Cycle whip on dominant side of body with weak hand (backhand Overhand Flick). After it cracks, cycle the whip around in a vertical circle on your dominant side until it is behind you, primed to throw forward again. Repeat 6 times.

Alternating sides (Swashbuckler cross cuts).

5) With dominant hand, throw whip forward so it cracks then cycle whip to opposite side and throw forward. Make the cracks occur at the same point directly in front of you, so the whip follows an X-shaped trajectory in front of you. Repeat 6 times.

6) With weak hand, throw whip forward so it cracks then cycle whip to opposite side and throw forward. Make the cracks occur at the same point directly in front of you, so the whip follows an X-shaped trajectory in front of you. Repeat 6 times.

C. Circus Crack

1) Draw whip forward and gently up with dominant hand on dominant side. Execute Circus Crack in front, then ground whip on your dominant side. Repeat 6 times.

2) Perform gentle Circus Crack on weak side of body with dominant hand. After it cracks, cycle the whip down to your weak side, grounding it. Repeat 6 times.

Switch hands.

3) Draw whip forward and gently up with weak hand on weak side. Execute Circus Crack in front, then ground whip on your weak side. Repeat 6 times.

4) Perform gentle Circus Crack on dominant side of body with weak hand. After it cracks, cycle the whip down to your dominant side, grounding it. Repeat 6 times.

D. Stockman's Crack

1) Draw whip forward and gently up with dominant hand on dominant side as if performing a Circus crack, but angle the whip's trajectory slightly over your head. Crack going away from you, and follow through outside your body. Repeat 6 times, increasing angle of attack slightly until the whole stroke is almost parallel to the ground.

Switch hands

2) Draw whip forward and gently up with weak hand on weak side, as if performing a Circus crack, but angle the whip's trajectory slightly over your head. Crack going away from you, and follow through outside your body. Repeat 6 times, increasing angle of attack slightly until the whole stroke is almost parallel to the ground.

BASIC BULLWHIP PRACTICE ROUTINE NO. 2
MULTIPLE CRACKS

(SingleWhip. For right-handed people, "dominant" side is right side; "weak" side is left side. For left-handed people, "dominant" side is left side; "weak" side is right side. Please wear eye protection.)

A. Slow Figure 8's
B. Fast Figure 8's

C. Volleys
D. Self Wraps

A. Slow Figure 8's

1) Align belly. Perform forward Circus Crack on dominant side. As you follow through, use this to swing the whip up into a Reverse Circus Crack. Realign belly. Use the sweep-through after this reverse crack to line the whip up for your next forward Circus Crack Repeat 6 times.

Switch Hands.

2) Align belly. With your weak hand, perform forward Circus Crack on weak side. As you follow through, realign belly and swing the whip up into a Reverse Circus Crack. Use the sweep-through after this reverse crack to line the whip up for your next forward Circus Crack. Repeat 6 times.

B. Fast Figure 8's

1) Align belly. Perform forward Circus Crack on dominant side. Immediately after it cracks and before it goes down in front of you, roll the whip handle backward without realigning the belly so it cracks again behind you. Follow through, swinging the whip down, forward and up so it is lined up to perform another Slow Figure 8.

2) Perform the same crack on your dominant side, but align belly to start the first crack behind you (Reverse Circus Crack). Roll the whip instantly forward and follow through from front to back along the ground, lifting the whip up behind you to begin next sequence of Slow Figure 8's.

Switch hands

3) Align belly and perform forward Circus Crack on weak side. Immediately after it cracks and before it goes down in front of you, roll the whip backward without realigning the belly so it cracks again behind you. Follow through, swinging the whip around, forward and up so it is lined up to perform another Slow Figure 8.

4) Perform the same crack on your weak side, but start with the first crack behind you (Reverse Circus Crack), roll the whip instantly forward and follow through from front to back along the ground, lifting the whip up behind you to begin next sequence of Slow Figure 8's.

C. Volleys

1) Perform volleys on dominant side. Start with one volley (one crack forward, one crack behind), then sweep whip underhand to rise to perform next volley. Repeat once.

2) Increase number of volley by one with each cycle. This means the second cycle will have three cracks and follow through in the same direction you started in. Repeat 3 times.

3) Perform a 4-crack volley, then a 6-crack volley. Increase number to 12 volleys (24 cracks)

Switch hands and repeat above.

D) Self Wraps

1) Align belly and with your dominant hand, throw a side shot forward so it cracks and comes around to your weak side *outside* your arm. Let the whip wrap your waist. Pull the whip handle up and follow the thong around you, repeating the sequence as a continuous cycle. Crack forward again into another non-locking waist wrap. Repeat 6 times.

2) Perform a backhand side shot with your dominant hand, coming from the weak side of your body outside your arm to crack and wrap your waist on your dominant side. Pull the whip's handle over your head, follow the rolling thong and crack ahead again, repeating the sequence as a continuous cycle. Repeat 6 times.

Switch hands.

3) Repeat #1 with your weak hand.

4) Repeat #2 with your weak hand.

Note: End each routine with a wrap that "locks," which means instead of allowing the thong to roll *outside* your arm, lift your arm so the goes *under* it to wrap your waist. Pull backward on the handle so it snugs down on your opposite shoulder, locking the whip in place around you.

SAFETY PROTOCOLS

These safety protocols were devised by Andrew Conway ("The Bullwhip Book") and are reprinted here with his kind permission. Make sure everyone reads and agrees to them.

Bullwhips can cut flesh, break bones, put out eyes and slice off ears. Treat all whips with respect and use these common sense safety precautions to limit damage to an occasional welt.

Protect Other People

Be aware of the space around you, including directly behind you and over your head. Allow plenty of room for your whip to crack.

Do not fool around with a whip or threaten anyone with it. Uncontrolled and unscripted use of a whip can have unpredictable results.

Never use a whip where it might pick up dirt or gravel or fling objects like pebbles at someone.

Protect Yourself

Wear protective clothing. Eye protection is mandatory. Gloves will prevent blisters on your hands. Ear plugs will make the sound level more comfortable. A stout jacket and pants may save you some welts. When you are not cracking, stay near the walls of the gym. Do not enter anyone else's space without warning them. Remember they may be wearing earplugs so make sure they acknowledge you.

Protect the Whips

Do not crack the whip too loudly. It is not only bad for the whip but also unpleasant for other people. True control of the whip means you can crack it as quietly as you like.

Do not use anyone else's whip without permission.

When you are not using the whip, do not leave it on the floor where someone might tread on it or trip over it.

_____

THE PERFECT WHIP THROW

I am still watching elegant ripples flow outward through my thoughts from an article I read last week about the seminal Beau Brummel, of all people. Cabinet Magazine featured an article by Brian Dillon titled "A Poet of the Cloth" in which he defines Brummel's approach to sartorial sophistication in words that could just as easily be applied to whip cracking. The parallels were beyond eerie - they were uncanny.

The discovery was serendipity: I was searching for source material to expand my knowledge of cravat tying in order to make my performing costumes sharper and more era-authentic at Wild West events.

Between cutting and sewing numerous works of neckwear, I was enjoying Dillon's analysis of H. Le Blanc's 1828 The Art of Tying the Cravat, a piece illustrated with such creations as the easy-going L'Americain cravat and the more sinuous and sensual Sentimentale. Some of the books cited went back to 1818, and many were written in the early 1920s and 1930s. In one paragraph, Dillon captured the essence of the art of cravat tying:

"What the wearer (of a cravat) is after is a 'curious mean' between skill and pure chance...the knot is intentional, but the folds are entirely fortuitous..."

These words exploded at me in a burst of light.

They highlighted to me the fact that contradictions abound in the realms of pure whip cracking. The perfect throw is often an unintended side effect. An apparent effortlessness in whip handling is usually the result of years of conscious and determined practice.

As a consequence of my immersion in the Marvelous, I am delighted that even with such a mundane activity as necktie tying, the principles of Power and Transformation (my personal household gods) combine to detonate an ordinary instant into an event of alchemical beauty, a moment validating the Divine that flows through us rather than from us, but which we can nonetheless experience and enjoy with and for ourselves, and with and for our audiences.

I was grateful for this postcard from the Universe. It reminded me that one should never, *ever* settle for mere Perfection.

WHIPS AS EXERCISE

I was asked, "Do you happen to know how many calories you burn up practicing with a bullwhip or during a show or session?"

This question intrigued me, so I used 20 minutes as my baseline for a 200-pound person. The best I could do was to compare various activities for the same amount of time, since the energy expenditure levels have such a large variance.

GENTLE WORKOUT EQUIVALENT

Stationary rowing, moderate	212 calories
Kayaking	151
Frisbee general	136
Golf: walking and pulling clubs	130
Tai Chi	121
Archery: non-hunting	106
Walking: 3 mph (20 min/mi)	100

PERFORMANCE EQUIVALENT

Martial Arts: judo, karate, tae kwan do	303 calories
Soccer	212
Fencing	180

This info was gleaned from http://www.primusweb.com/cgi-bin/fpc/actcalc.pl

The length of a whip and consequently, its weight also makes a difference. If you do a two-handed workout instead of a single-whip workout, the results will be higher.

I love getting questions like this because they make me think more intently about what I do, and that adds to my enjoyment of cracking whips. It's sort of like reading the score as you listen to a symphony.

ONE DOZEN WAYS TO IMPROVE ACCURACY

Most people make the same mistakes, not only when they start out but also when they are well along in the whip cracking experience.

One question that comes up is again and again is how to improve one's accuracy using a whip to shoot targets.

One of these standard solutions might help you to solve the problem of being more accurate with a whip.

1. Check your whip. Look for tiny tangles or knots in the fall and cracker. Make sure your whip is conditioned so it will roll smoothly. Pay special attention to the fall, because this will need more greasing than the thong.

2. Use a sword-fighter stance. This will align your whole body with the throw and end the problems caused by torqueing your body and the whip.

3. Hold the whip's handle parallel to your body. Keep your arm extended along a vertical line so you are able to aim straight down your arm, hand and handle. Go slow, with enough oomph to keep the whip in the air.

4. Remember that all throws begin *behind* you. With the Overhand Flick, hoist whip behind you a bit higher than your shoulder so you are throwing slightly downhill by a few inches. This automatically increases accuracy.

5. Use the "Point and Squeeze" technique at the point of the pop. Use the Overhand Flick for a precise throw at a point in space. The Circus Crack is good for cutting down a straight line. It is not as good for depth work.

6. Remember the depth of your specific crack. The Overhand Flick cracks at the end of the fully extended whip, but the Circus Crack cracks 2/3 to 3/4 of the length of the whip. The depths are different for these two cracks, even though they are consistent in themselves.

7. Use the belly of the whip to your advantage. The whip wants to roll along its belly-spine axis. If your throw is off the line of the belly, or if your hand torques the whip off line, it will flip and flop at the end of the crack.

8. Go slower. A muscled whip is not accurate. You still get the power you want if you exaggerate movement. Go Big, Go Slow.

9. Use shorter whips. You stand closer to your target.

10. When outside, note the wind direction. It might not seem like much to you, but that little cracker can become a kite in a gale at the end of your fall.

11. Compensate. Pick a target and throw the whip. See how far you miss and in what direction. Compensate exactly this amount for your following throws. Usually, you need do this only a few times, particularly at the beginning of a practice or performance. Sometimes it's your form but sometimes it's the whip itself. For example, your whip may be retaining its memory of how it was coiled and stored. Just as you need to warm up, your whip does, as well.

12. Relax your ass. No kidding! It's a very effective dancer's trick, because when you take a deep breath and let go of the stress and tension in your buttocks, your whole body relaxes. And all that is communicated into the whip.

CHOREOGRAPHY: WRITE IT OUT!

Here's an example for you, an entire performance which uses a dozen long-stemmed red roses and a candle as the only props:

Assistant enters with a dozen long-stemmed red roses. She peels down a few petals seductively and holds the flower out. Dante knocks the petals off the flower. She peels more petals and they quickly follow the first petals, fluttering to the floor in the wake of the cracks. Assistant picks the petals up and drops them, one by one, as Dante cracks them out of mid-air.

The second rose fares no better, as she turns her back to the audience and clenches the stem between her thighs and leans forward. After caressing it gently with the whip, Dante lops the head off the rose. (This trick is called Spanking the Monkey.)

Assistant holds the third rose in the air over her head as she drops to one knee. A horizontal stroke sends the rose's head flying. (Safety Note: Aim away from the audience so the rose does not fly into the crowd.)

The fourth, fifth and sixth roses are held as a bunch, and Dante's slicing circus crack splits through the roses in a red shower of flower petals like an explosion of blood.

Assistant picks up several of the petals and places them in little piles on her outstretched arm. Dante's crack is close enough to blow the petals off her arm without touching her. (Note: this uses the Point and Squeeze technique to make whip crack before it contacts skin. Done right, it does not injure or mark.)

The seventh rose is held in the her teeth. A crack close to her face sends the head of the flower rolling, another victim of the bullwhip's lash. (Note: Tina performed this with Conan O'Brien on the late Night Show. Brava, Tina!)

The eighth and ninth roses extend out behind Assistant as she clenches the stems under her arms like double-handed swagger sticks. The whip reduces the flowers to petals, inches from her back.

The tenth rose which the Assistant presents holds a candle which Dante snuffs.

Assistant stands with her arms extended, a rose in each hand. Dante wraps her arms, legs and waist with the whip. She extends one rose to her side and Dante uses the whip to wrap and grab it, pulling it to himself. As he sniffs it luxuriously, Assistant steps toward Dante, savoring the aroma of her own flower. Dante holds his flower to his side, and Assistant holds hers out. Dante wraps her waist. She spins to tighten the wrap and pulls herself into his embrace as they lift their roses to the audience together.

End

From Dante's Notebook: I use a shorthand system. Here's an outline for a show with dialogue and anecdotes, written so I can grasp it at a glance. It helps to put it like this when I visualize a show and then walk through it so I get it not only in my mind but in my body's muscle memory. Musicians use set lists taped to the backs of their instruments. A detailed breakdown will have the timing written out.

> ***Shooters Roundup***
> ***Music – Action- Props***
> 1 Trailer Tunes - Seating-warm up-greeting
> 2 Western Streets - whips-mach one- 3 whips
> 3 Sting 1 - Tina intro
> 4 sting 2 - Tina solo
> 5 Gold Rush 1 - balloon miss 1 - balloons
> 6 Hand Trolley Song - card trick- deck, large card
> 7 Shanty Song - poi – newspaper- poi – newspaper
> 8 Waltz- mirror cut - flower – mirror
> 9 Gold Rush 2 - balloon miss 2- balloon
> 10 Smoking gun - dinosaur story- snake whip – maracas
> 11 Tango - Whip duet
> 12 Dangerous - Swashbucklers
> 13 Penn Rose - farewells, advertising
> 14 Gold Rush 3 - balloon hit 3- balloons
> 15 Whip Song - Finale

Believe it or not, this is a guide to create a 20-minute show. Use the musical cues to know where you are, where you should be, and what's coming up next.

AFTERWARD

My urge is to apologize for everything I've said here. If I'd taken 10 years to rewrite and polish the prose, it would have been a better book, but it also would have been finished 10 years from now. And the need is NOW for a book like this.

All I can promise you is that I am always making additions and corrections to this text. Lord knows I could have made a book as long as this one with the material I took out in order to make this one a reasonable length. For example, I would love to talk about some of the interesting physics of dinosaur tails. Ah, well, next time... ("Cue the Apatosaurus!")

I hope this book is useful to you. Feel free to write in it. It's *your* manual. I genuinely hope you heed its ongoing exhortations to observe safety parameters.

Of course, I do not have all the answers. No one person does. But if you are looking for some other perspectives or for credible resources for whips, there are plenty in the world. Take what you can use and just file the rest away for later.

Trust your whip. It does not lie. It can't.

The bullwhip has been good to me. *Very* good to me, in fact. The more I have served it, the more it has served me. It has unfolded and stretched before me as a sinuous Road to the Absolute.

It has been uncompromising in its honest and immediate feedback. Its direct reality has both grounded me and led me for years, and while I run the risk of sounding arrogant, it is my fervent desire to do it honor by sharing with you what I know of it. In essence, this is the book I wish I'd had when I was beginning.

But book is not an encyclopedia. It is not a comprehensive reference work, and it certainly is not the last word on the subject.

This book is essentially a "grimoire" for every Sorcerer's Apprentice who wants to pick up a whip like a wand and create magic.

Admittedly, the word "grimoire" usually means an encyclopedia of western magic, including spells and incantations. My choice of this word is deliberate for while I am wary of "going California" and seeing cosmic truths in banalities, I agree with metaphysical author Dion Fortune's definition of Magic as the art of changing consciousness at will. In short, Magic is Power — and for me, the bullwhip is Power made conscious and tangible. Each crack is a wake-up call, an affirmation, every throw a step in a dance of life and death, at the same instant glorious, graceful and terrifying. Further, it's sexy, it's scary, it's dangerous — and it's fun.

So, here is the book to serve the young whipper-snapper, the Sorcerer's Apprentice, the first-time tyro. I also hope this is a book against which other masters of the bullwhip may compare their knowledge with an eye to making future editions more accurate and useful to others.

I do not pretend to have created any of the material in this book any more than Edison "invented" electricity. All I have done is to pull together what I have learned from others and been taught by my own direct experience with the bullwhip. To keep things in perspective, this book is only one man's perspective on the ancient and still evolving art of the bullwhip, and in this world there are many people well qualified to address this subject. The advent of the Internet has made these people immediately accessible to anyone with a keyboard and a modem. Some are expert handlers, some are whip braiders and some are top-notch teachers. Most are workers while some rare ones are wizards — but with only a few exceptions, they all have something to share and teach and most are well worth searching out.

Obviously, I've written this book from a whip cracker's perspective, not a whip maker's. We have had several excellent books written by plaiters and whip makers about how to braid whips, but too few on how to handle them. Even today, there is only one other credible book easily available in the United States which addresses whip cracking itself, and that is the one written by Andrew Conway, "The Bullwhip Book." It is a measure of his generosity that he has been so helpful in the writing of this volume.

I've tried to keep this presentation simple and easy to understand, but the experience was daunting for a long time. There were many false starts, but patience and persistence can be a powerful combination in any endeavor. I've had to weigh the need for this book against the desire to take a decade to complete it, and if there are errors in this version, I hope I will have the chance to correct them or to make additions in future editions.

Talking about whips is always difficult because there is no universally recognized nomenclature for cracks or even whips. Often, the differences between differently named whips and cracks are maddeningly minuscule (try to get an experienced whip cracker to accurately tell you the difference between a Gypsy Crack, a Circus Crack and a Stockman's Crack, and you'll see what I mean). There are not even comparable standards of measurement between different types of whips.

Whip enthusiasts worldwide do not share a common vocabulary, but I've spoken with experienced coaches, leather braiders and performers about their experiences with bullwhips. Without exception, we were able to communicate and understand each other because this is a language based in experience, not theory.

In other words, a book like this could never have been written alone. I wish I could thank each person who has contributed to this effort, but my list, for all its length would be, regrettably and unavoidably, incomplete because I have learned something new from every person I have taught or with whom I have cracked whips.

Some are masters whose names are well known and here I wish to acknowledge them.

I thank the great whip maker and champion cracker Mike Murphy, the amazing Peter Jack, pioneering Mark Allen, redoubtable Alex Green, the revered Russel Schultz, ever-faithful Sharron Taylor from Eskaytee Whipmakers, whip maker Simon Martin, Jim Hurlbut, Dan Speaker, Rhett Kelley and Guy Baldwin for patiently and passionately talking to me about our shared enthusiasm for single-tail whips.

I thank the late Ken Fontenot, Col. Niabow, and Michael A., for first opening my eyes to what was possible with a bullwhip years ago in Houston, Texas. I thank Chris Wiggins and Brenda Fogg for their faith, their friendship, and a shared passion for sushi.

Philip Miller and Molly Devon are to be thanked for first encouraging me to commit my thoughts to paper. And patient Molly should be thanked again for encouraging me to complete this project.

I thank Jay Wagner of Toronto for being the first person to ask me to bring my whips to a fundraiser, whetting an appetite in me to pursue a career as a bullwhip artist.

I thank John Brady (and Vi) for setting the standard and blazing a trail around the globe which others now follow. I thank Alan Fox for helping me to create the ground-breaking video, "Bullwhip: Art of the Single Tail Whip." I sincerely thank Loup and Jan of Portland for their steadfast friendship in whip craft.

150

I thank everyone who ever attended a practice sponsored by the Los Angeles Whip Enthusiasts. I also thank the incredible attendees of The Minneapolis Bullwhip Academy who braved hell, high water and snow drifts to join me cracking whips in studios in the Twin Cities.

I thank Drew, Dorothy M., Stephanie, Don Bastian, Karen Quest, Joyce Rice, Mitch Herman (and Kathleen), Manon (and Jessica), and Rob M. for sharing their time and invaluable insights with me.

I thank Mark Shuler, a man who knows there need be no discrepancy between sensitivity and courage, who helped me cross the Rubicon to my first Guinness World Record.

I thank those whose names I have forgotten, even to the 5-year-old kids who showed me things I hadn't seen before.

I wish to thank my second wife, Mary (now Mary DeLongis), who for years shared my art, my passion, the rigors of the road, the risks and the rewards entailed in bringing the magic of the bullwhip before the world and dancing intimately with me in the heart of the whip's wind.

I wish to thank Kim Cochran for her faith, encouragement, and infectious enthusiasm, expressed in leonine fashion in her performances with me before audiences, young and old. She gave unstintingly and unselfishly in her desire to experience, explore, and share with others the mystery and mirth of the variety artist's high.

I wish to thank again Andrew Conway, whose own book, "The Bullwhip Book," has helped this art and sport reach a wider audience. His patient, painstaking reading of my manuscript and his suggestions (especially in the chapters on performing) were invaluable. Happily, he is as good a teacher as he is a friend so I count myself doubly blessed to know him. Thank you, Andrew!

I thank Paul McDonald, whose sharp-eyed reading encouraged me to improve the quality of the final version of this book. I also thank Carl Bergstrom for helping me to

I thank Gery Deer (a true gentleman, entertainer and teacher) for his generosity and respect, and I thank Chris Camp (The Whip Guy) for his stolid camaraderie. I thank Mike Woolridge for epitomizing all that's good and true about "The Cowboy Way."

I especially thank Brian Chic for his friendship and for reminding me teaching must be a two-way street to have any value.

I wish to thank Drs. John Bartlett, Michael Walsh andMelissa Nesdahl, who restored my faith in medicine when they helped me through a frozen shoulder episode. I thank Dr. Sharon Young, whose voice I still hear in moments of lucidity and compassion. I thank my father, the RAF navigator who taught me how to look at the stars; I thank my mother, who showed me how to make a cup of tea as though this mundane act held secrets of profound meaning (it does!); I thank my brother Ronald, a modern day buccaneer; I thank Allen Ginsberg who gave me friendship and good advice (to this day I think he should have been awarded a Nobel Prize for so many different and legitimate reasons); and I thank Nutmeg, a little fellow who showed me the meaning of 'unconditional love,' and that without it, no one can hope to fully embrace the human experience.

And I especially thank Tina Nagy without whom this book would not have been finished and to whom it is dedicated, with my profound gratitude, respect and love.

A book, a hands-on lesson or a good video can teach technique but it cannot communicate that intangible 'spirit of the whip.'

Perhaps, someday, when you are cracking your whip under the blue sky in your back yard, you may relax and throw an unconscious forward Flick that amazes you with its purity and clean power. Your motion will be effortless, but the intensity you will feel will be tremendous. At this moment, some inner light bulb inside you may turn on and you may instantly understand the intangible experience I have tried to express between the lines of this book.

It's an Open Secret, as Rumi said. The Magic is around you, and in your hand, waiting for you to free it and for it to free you.

A good book is written backwards, from the future to the present. If this effort falls short on any level, I hope it will at least point you in the right direction and give you practical and pragmatic tools to accomplish your journey. Like any map it is a guide, and the guide is never the journey itself. That's up to you.

Any and all credit must go to the names listed above; any faults found in here are my own. Because the more I learn, the more I know that I am still learning, too. A good teacher never stops being a student. And a good Magician must never believe he knows it all.

Respectfully,
Robert Dante

About the Author

Robert Dante is a three-time Guinness World Record holder (Most Bullwhip Cracks in One Minute), and 2008 recipient of the Brian Chic Whip Artistry award given by the Society of American Whip Artistry. Dante founded the LA Whip Enthusiasts whip cracking club and The Bullwhip Academy in Minneapolis. He has appeared on numerous TV programs and stories about him have appeared in newspapers and magazines. His website is at www.bullwhip.net. As an author, Dante has published 100 poems, 300 non-fiction articles, two books and a film script. He collects museum-quality Zeppelin memorabilia.

About Tina

Tina (Nagy) brings together different disciplines in her wealth of artistic experience. She is a professional belly dancer in the Twin Cities, both as a soloist and with the Jawaahir Dance Company. As a Target Girl for a knife thrower, she has appeared in several television programs including America's Got Talent (Season 2), the History Channel's "Modern Marvels," Univision's "Don Francisco Presenta" and "Late Night with Conan O'Brien," where the trusting talk show host placed a flower in his clenched teeth for her to cut with a 6-foot bullwhip. She also works as a professional magician's assistant with Chris Winter.

Her blog at EmpoweredVulnerability.com explores the concept of "Dancing on the Edge" as Tina experiences it in the tradition of Target Girls, magician's assistants, daredevils, wing walkers, whip assistants and other Sorcerer's Apprentices. A whip cracker and performer in her own right, Tina gives lessons and performs with bullwhips with Dante and as a solo act. She enjoys competitive knitting (mostly competing with her cats), aerial arts and cooking. She has made it her personal mission to dispel the belief that accountants lead boring lives.

INDEX

155

THE DARING TINA

Visit www.empoweredvulnerability.com

Visit www.bullwhip.net

28157263R00090

Made in the USA
Charleston, SC
02 April 2014